D0065212

Modern Language Association of America

Options for Teaching

Joseph Gibaldi, Series Editor

1. *Options for the Teaching of English: The Undergraduate Curriculum.* Edited by Elizabeth Wooten Cowan. 1975.
2. *Options for the Teaching of English: Freshman Composition.* Edited by Jasper P. Neel. 1978.
3. *Options for Undergraduate Foreign Language Programs: Four-Year and Two-Year Colleges.* By Renate A. Schulz. 1979.
4. *The Teaching Apprentice Program in Language and Literature.* Edited by Joseph Gibaldi and James V. Mirollo. 1981.
5. *Film Study in the Undergraduate Curriculum.* Edited by Barry K. Grant. 1983.
6. *Part-Time Academic Employment in the Humanities: A Sourcebook for Just Policy.* Edited by M. Elizabeth Wallace. 1984.
7. *Teaching Environmental Literature: Materials, Methods, Resources.* Edited by Frederick O. Waage. 1985
8. *School-College Collaborative Programs in English.* Edited by Ron Fortune. 1986.

School-College Collaborative Programs in English

Edited by

Ron Fortune

The Modern Language Association of America
New York   1986

Copyright © 1986 by The Modern Language Association of America

Library of Congress Cataloging-in-Publication Data

Main entry under title:

School-college collaborative programs in English.
    (Options for teaching; 8)
    Bibliography: p.
    1—English philology—Study and teaching (Higher)—United States—Addresses, essays, lectures. 2. English philology—Study and teaching (Secondary)—United States—Addresses, essays, lectures. 3. English language—Rhetoric—Study and teaching—United States—Addresses, essays, lectures. 4. English language—Composition and exercises—Study and teaching—United States—Addresses, essays, lectures. 5. Articulation (Education)—United States—Addresses, essays, lectures.
    I. Fortune, Ron, 1948-
PE68.U5S36   1986   428'.007'1173   86-711
ISBN 0-87352-360-1
ISBN 0-87352-361-X (pbk.)

Published by the Modern Language Association of America
10 Astor Place, New York, NY 10003

Contents

Introduction   vii

Georgetown University: The Articulation Program and Related Projects
James F. Slevin   1

Bard College: Institute for Writing and Thinking
Paul Connolly   8

Yale University: Yale–New Haven Teachers Institute
James R. Vivian   14

Queens College, CUNY: The Queens English Project
Donald McQuade and Sandra Schor   25

University of California, Berkeley: The Bay Area Writing Project and the National Writing Project
James Gray   35

Miami University (Ohio): The Ohio Writing Project–Early English Composition Assessment Program
Mary Fuller and Max Morenberg   46

Youngstown State University: The English Festival and Project ARETE
Barbara Brothers, Carol Gay, Gratia Murphy, and Gary Salvner   52

University of Southern California: The Huntington Beach Project Literacy
W. Ross Winterowd   61

National Endowment for the Humanities: Humanities Instruction in Elementary and Secondary Schools Program
Carolynn Reid-Wallace   70

University of Illinois, Urbana-Champaign: University Associates in Rhetoric Program
R. Baird Shuman   80

University of Michigan: The Outreach Program of the English Composition Board
Jay L. Robinson and Patricia L. Stock   86

National Endowment for the Humanities: Summer Seminars for Secondary School Teachers
Ronald Herzman   92

Gonzaga University: National Endowment for the Humanities Summer Seminar: The Quest for Love and Knowledge
Franz Schneider   97

Utah State University: Northern Utah's English Articulation Program
Joyce Kinkead, William Smith, and Pat Stoddart   105

Illinois State University: The Cooperative Teaching Program
Ron Fortune and Janice Neuleib   111

Skidmore College: Cooperative Program in Cross-Curricular Writing
Philip P. Boshoff   120

Works Cited   127

Introduction

High school English teachers must surely rank among the most beleaguered groups in American education. A host of recent reports on secondary education have charged that many high school graduates lack the verbal skills they should have acquired in their English courses. A 1983 report of the United States Department of Education's National Commission on Excellence in Education concludes that the schools often fail to provide students with the reading and writing skills needed to succeed in college and, beyond that, in life itself (9). A study of writing instruction in American secondary schools further asserts that most existing programs are doomed to "certain failure" (Cooper xi). But perhaps the most perplexing criticism has come from college and university English professors, who commonly lament, "What are they teaching in high schools today? My students can neither write a decent essay nor respond to a poem or a short story with any degree of insight!" Such comments are perplexing because the concern they suggest has not always been reflected in the readiness of college English professors to work with their high school counterparts. Although closer cooperation between high school and college English teachers seems an obvious way to improve the quality of both secondary and postsecondary English instruction, until recently few universities and high schools have actively cultivated collaborative programs.

Fortunately, the many recent studies of American secondary education have produced a new emphasis on cooperation between secondary and postsecondary teachers. Addressing a 1980 conference on higher education, Ernest Boyer, president of the Carnegie Foundation for the Advancement of Teaching, expressed the pressing need to move in this direction: "In recent years the relationship between the colleges and schools has been essentially ignored. Presidents and deans refuse to talk to principals and district superintendents. College faculty refuse to meet with their counterparts in the public schools. And curriculum reforms at each level are planned in total isolation" (qtd. in Watkins 1). At about the same time, Allan Ostar, the executive director of the American Association of State Colleges and Universities, insisted that efforts aimed at bridging the gap between high school and college instruction should receive highest priority (qtd. in Watkins 14). Accordingly, educators throughout the country have begun to look for ways to connect secondary and postsecondary education more effectively. During the summer of 1983, for example, the presidents of six major universities (Harvard University, Stanford University, University of Chicago, University of Wisconsin, University of Michigan, and Columbia University) met to outline some of the activities colleges and universities should undertake to strengthen their connections to secondary schools ("Six University Presidents" 5).

Much of this interest in collaborative activities has focused on the importance of getting secondary and postsecondary English teachers to work together. The Rockefeller Commission on the Humanities advocated coordinating secondary school and college writing instruction because, they argued, writing must be learned through "constant practice and the sequential development of skills"

(54). And some professional groups have stressed the need for similar coopera-tion to improve the teaching and learning of literature in the nation's schools and colleges. Noting that students' "receptiveness to literature" and "some of their most fundamental intellectual attitudes" are shaped in high school, the Modern Language Association's Commission on the Future of the Profession recently urged high school and college literature teachers to interact with one another more thoroughly for their mutual benefit (528).

History

To suggest that high school and college English teachers have completely ignored one another over the years would, of course, misrepresent the case. In fact, they may have a better history of cooperation than do high school and college teachers in most other subject areas. A look back more than a quarter of a century to the Conference on Basic Issues in the Teaching of English in 1958 reveals that the call for more effective cooperation between high school and college English teachers is not a new phenomenon. Concerned with the fragmentation of En-glish studies at all grade levels, members of the conference developed a detailed plan for coordinating and focusing the teaching and learning of English across the grade levels, a plan that depended heavily on the interaction of elementary, secondary, and postsecondary English teachers. Reflecting the premise that the processes of learning to read literature and learning to write are "sequential and incremental," the plan that emerged from the conference specified the appropri-ate content for English courses from elementary school all the way through col-lege ("An Articulated English Program" 13-17). Moreover, it suggested specific activities that would increase interaction among English teachers at all levels so that the content called for in the plan could work its way into the curriculum most expeditiously.

Soon after the Conference on Basic Issues in the Teaching of English com-pleted its report, the National Council of Teachers of English Committee on High School–College Articulation issued a series of three position papers that dis-cussed everything from what colleges expected of high school graduates to the problems faced by existing school-college cooperative programs. One of these reports, "High School–College Liaison Programs: Sponsors, Patterns, and Prob-lems," broke down the various kinds of cooperative programs in place in the early 1960s. The most widespread of these programs included (1) annual or semi-annual conferences on problems shared by schools and colleges, (2) the inter-change of high school and college students and faculty, and (3) consultation between high school and college faculty on curricular issues (89-92). All these programs were sponsored locally by neighboring high schools and colleges, but part of what sustained them was a visible national effort to bridge secondary and postsecondary education in English.

Furthering the impetus gained from the Conference on Basic Issues in the Teaching of English and from the NCTE Committee on High School–College Articulation, the establishment of the Commission on English contributed to the national interest in school-college cooperation. This commission was created in 1959 by the College Board and consisted of school and college teachers whose professional affiliations included the Modern Language Association (MLA), the

National Council of Teachers of English (NCTE), the Conference on College Composition and Communication (CCCC), the National Education Association (NEA), and the Secondary Education Board. The commission published two reports—*College Preparation in English* (Oct. 1960) and *Preparation in English for College-Bound Students* (Nov. 1960)—that addressed, among other things, the effective integration of high school and college English curricula. In 1961 the commission sponsored an institute at the University of Michigan in which sixty representatives from twenty colleges collaboratively developed materials for retraining English teachers. The following summer, each of the participating colleges hosted a summer institute using the materials developed the previous year. Forty-five high school English teachers attended each of the institutes and received both graduate credit and stipends for their efforts. Not only did this plan coordinate secondary and postsecondary English teaching, but it also increased the consistency of postsecondary English programs. The representatives from the twenty colleges had to agree among themselves on an agenda for English education before they could present their ideas to teachers at the high school institutes.

In an essay on the state of school-college cooperation in the early sixties, Robert Rogers surveyed the extensive efforts in this area and outlined what he saw as a bright future for articulation programs. A passage from this essay captures the widespread optimism about the imminent successes of such programs during this period:

> Clearly patterns of cooperation already developed will be used more extensively than ever before. We will see more exchange appointments, with secondary school teachers holding visiting appointments on college faculties. Colleges will make more appointments of persons who have as a part of their responsibilities liaison work with the schools. . . . New patterns of cooperation are going to develop. The colleges will devise new plans for extension work, and the electronic media will come to be used in the work of instruction and cooperation. . . . The colleges may develop demonstration classrooms or centers. Certainly there must be, and will be, more effective liaison with various kinds of supervisory personnel.   (373)

The optimism reflected in this passage resulted in part from the recent passage of an expanded version of the National Defense Education Act. The funds that would become available to schools and colleges throughout the country seemed finally to provide the support needed to carry out so many aspects of the plan for active cooperation that had evolved during the 1950s. As important as this support was, however, schools and colleges did not begin these programs simply because necessary funds had finally become available. The most crucial reason was a dogged determination to bridge the separation between secondary and postsecondary English education.

Although school-college cooperation was not as prominent an issue during the subsequent decade, it did not completely disappear. At Dartmouth College in 1966, for example, the Anglo-American Conference on the Teaching of English stressed the ongoing need for such cooperation. In his account of the Dartmouth seminar, as the conference came to be called, John Dixon articulated the conferees' concern: "Current experiments in the closer working of school and college deserve careful study: we badly need to find the best ways of integrating professional education" (110). But, while many of these local and regional articulation programs continued to function, the national commitment and, to a degree, the local and regional commitment to improve school-college interaction lost much of its intensity. A symptom of this decline was the relatively little attention given to the issue in the professional journals at the time.

The change in the status of articulation programs reflected the changes that colleges and universities were undergoing during this decade. As enrollments began to rise in the early sixties, postsecondary institutions found that they had to concentrate their resources more and more on immediate campus needs. A whole range of issues kept colleges and universities from maintaining their commitment to work with secondary schools. Gene Maeroff's description of the fate of school-college cooperative programs in the sixties indicates what happened to articulation programs in English:

> During the 1960s, cooperation came to a screeching halt. New priorities came crashing in. Colleges and universities were caught up in the free speech movement, marches, sit-ins, teach-ins and other protests over Cambodia and Kent State.
> The Civil Rights movement pushed colleges to expand educational opportunities for minorities and women, and school districts were preoccupied with compensatory education and the challenge of desegregation. Concerns about academic excellence, curriculum continuity, and school-college collaboration were forgotten.
> Like lapsed lovers who had more important things to do, high schools and colleges stopped communicating with each other. They complained in each case that their efforts were unappreciated by the other.   (*School and College* 2–3)

With a variety of new needs competing for attention, university faculty and administrators understandably attended to those most visible and most pressing.

By the midseventies, however, with the "priorities" of the preceding decade beginning to lose momentum, signs of significant cooperation among secondary and postsecondary English teachers began to reemerge as the negative consequences of abandoned articulation programs became startlingly evident. The most significant of these consequences was the growth of remedial writing programs in colleges and universities across the country. (In a recent survey of 1,269 colleges and universities, the Instructional Resource Center at the City University of New York found that nine out of every ten schools now offer remedial writing courses.) As postsecondary English departments found more and more of their resources being absorbed by "precollege" writing courses, they realized that working with high school English teachers to combat the problem would have to become a high priority. At the same time, because the "literacy crisis" in America attracted national publicity, public and private funding agencies began to underwrite cooperative programs designed to improve the teaching and learning of writing in high school and college.

At present, school-college cooperation is beginning to regain the status it had twenty years ago. The most significant indicator of its renewed importance is the emergence of national organizations and national programs concerned with promoting work in this area. As noted earlier, the MLA's Commission on the Future of the Profession identified greater school-college cooperation as one of the profession's major needs. In its "Working Paper," the commission resolved to establish a liaison project with eight objectives directly or indirectly concerned with improving the relationship between secondary and postsecondary English teachers. Two of these objectives are especially noteworthy: (1) the liaison project would "determine how the MLA can best establish and maintain mutually beneficial relations with the teachers and organizations representing secondary schools" (536); (2) the project would "identify and publicize successful cooperative ventures between colleges and secondary schools for improving the teaching and learning of English and foreign languages" (536). The MLA has already begun to pursue both of these objectives. The first is evident in the current series of meetings, begun in the summer of 1984, in which the Coalition of English Associations—comprising officers and representatives of the Modern Language Association, the National Council of Teachers of English, the Conference on College Composition and Communication, the Association of Departments of English, the College Language Association, the College English Association, and the Conference on English Education—discuss strategies for collectively improving the teaching of English in high school and college through greater collaboration and other means. The second objective is reflected in the present collection of essays and in the panels on school-college collaborative projects included on the program of the MLA's annual convention for the past several years.

The College Board has also started to direct its energies toward improving communication between secondary and postsecondary teachers. In November 1983 representatives from thirteen collaborative programs around the country met at the College Board "to share their experiences and define the role of their new network in achieving equity and excellence in education" ("EQuality Project" 1). Among the several represented programs that bring high school and college English teachers together were those of the National Humanities Faculty and the Yale–New Haven Teachers Institute. The programs involved in this meeting were selected because of their potential as models or prototypes of school-college collaboration that can be readily adapted by schools and colleges nationally.

The National Endowment for the Humanities has also done its part to promote school-college collaboration in the humanities. It sponsors two programs—the Summer Institutes for Teachers and the Summer Seminars for Secondary School Teachers—that encourage high school and college English teachers to share their approaches to teaching writing and literature. Both programs have been successful because they begin by solving what often proves the most difficult problem in achieving high school–college collaboration: they provide the funds needed to cover the costs of the institutes and seminars.

A program that has had an especially widespread impact on the emergence of English articulation projects nationwide is the Bay Area Writing Project. This project began in 1974 at the University of California, Berkeley, when administrators at the university became concerned over the poor writing abilities of entering freshmen. The project organized intensive summer institutes that brought together elementary through secondary school writing teachers to analyze their own writing processes and to hear successful peers explain effective techniques for teaching writing. Initially limited to the immediate needs of the university and schools in its vicinity, the project grew in a few years into the National Writing Project and now serves as a model of articulation for 141 colleges and universities in 45 states. This level of participation reflects not only the adaptability of the program—a characteristic of most effective collaborative programs—but also the eagerness of secondary and postsecondary English teachers to work together when they have an effective model to follow.

The programs described above, the many national conferences on articulation conducted each year (e.g., the conference of school superintendents and college presidents sponsored by the Carnegie Foundation for the Advancement of Teaching in 1982 and the National Conference on Higher Education in February 1984), and the various recent reports stressing the importance of school-college collaboration have all helped to reestablish a national climate in which cooperative efforts can once again flourish. This national emphasis, as noted earlier, is crucial to sustaining collaborative projects at local and regional levels. It seems particularly important that the English-teaching profession recognize the lapses of recent history and take the necessary steps to ensure that they are not repeated. The greatest threat to the current projects is that the national commitment to school-college cooperation will once again dissipate and thus deprive local and regional efforts of the support they need if they are to succeed.

Programs

In an essay describing a small collection of school-college cooperative programs around the country, Michael O'Keefe, vice-president of the Carnegie Foundation for the Advancement of Teaching, outlined the various ways in which secondary and postsecondary teachers typically work together (5). The following survey of general trends in English articulation programs modifies only slightly O'Keefe's categories, largely because the focus here is specifically on one discipline rather than on all academic areas. According to the categories used here, most English articulation programs attempt to do one of three things: (1) to facilitate the movement of students from one educational level to the next, (2) to improve the quality of teaching and learning in secondary schools through curriculum development, or (3) to establish stronger professional ties between high school and college teachers. While these functions are not mutually exclusive, individual programs can be classified according to which of the three they emphasize most.

The most common approach to facilitating the matriculation from high school to college consists of offering college English courses on a high school campus or of enabling high school students to enroll in English courses at a college campus. A survey conducted by the Carnegie Foundation for the Advancement of Teaching showed that about 260 programs of this kind are in place throughout the country and that they enroll approximately 28,000 students (Boyer, *High School* 260). Many of the programs that pursue the first of these two strategies do not limit themselves to English courses but instead try to cover as large a curricular area as possible. Syracuse University's Project Advance, which offers college courses at high school campuses, is one of the most widely publicized programs of this kind. It covers several disciplines and involves seventy-six high schools from four states. In this program, high school teachers who have the credentials to teach entry-level courses in college teach at their high school campuses the same courses offered to entering freshmen at Syracuse. They use the same textbooks and the same course material found in the courses at the university. The high school students receive the same credit for each completed course that they would if they had been enrolled at the Syracuse campus. The project allows for regular communication between high school and college instructors who teach the same courses, a policy that ensures the equivalency of the courses at the high school and at the university and that encourages greater cooperation between the high school and university teachers.

Having high school instructors teach the college courses at their own schools is a less common practice than having college faculty members travel to the high school campuses to teach these courses. When teachers from a nearby college or university visit a high school campus to give a college course for which students receive college credit, the school also generally sets up opportunities for its own faculty members to interact with the college instructors. For example, the visiting instructors may conduct in-service workshops or serve as consultants for program reviews. While this approach to school-college articulation can be useful, it nonetheless sacrifices an important advantage of programs such as Syracuse's Project Advance. When high school instructors teach the college courses, they not only provide their students with an opportunity for accelerated learning but also learn themselves, through firsthand experience, much more about course planning and curriculum development than they could from in-service workshops or program reviews alone. The resulting articulation is thus more deep-seated and pervasive than it would be if the high school teachers were less directly involved in the college course.

Some colleges now use electronic media to give local high school students the opportunity to take college courses. A program at Indiana University–Purdue University, Indianapolis, for example, uses television to teach college composition and college literature courses to high school students. University instructors remain on their campus to teach the courses, while the students at their respective high schools attend through a television hookup. In 1985, six Indianapolis high schools were participating in the program, with students from all six taking a given course at the same time. To counter the impersonal factor introduced by the electronic media, this program specifically allows students to communicate with one another and with the university teacher during class time.

The program uses an audiointeractive system: each classroom contains two or more telephones; at the start of each class, the instructor places a conference call to each school, allowing students to use the hookup to participate in class discussions or to ask questions of the teacher. So far, the program has offered two freshman composition courses and two introductory literature courses.

One approach to facilitating the transition from high school to college has focused on identifying the areas in which students must improve their writing skills while still in high school. In 1983, for example, the Ohio Board of Regents announced that it would make funds available to support an Early English Composition Assessment Program. Under this program, Ohio high schools and state-supported universities receive funds to test the writing skills of eleventh-grade students. The test results provide a basis for advising students about the work they need to complete in composition before graduating from high school. This program reduces the need for remedial work in composition in Ohio's colleges and universities by ensuring that students graduate from high school with the skills that college work requires. In addition, it allows high school and college teachers to alter high school writing curricula to accommodate what test results reveal about student needs at the individual schools. In fact, Youngstown State University and Miami University in Ohio have integrated their findings into already existing educational programs for high school teachers.

The cooperative programs that stress improving the quality of teaching and learning in secondary schools typically focus on improving curriculum through intensive workshops or seminars. The most widespread example of this approach in English is the National Writing Project. One of the project's several distinguishing features is its insistence on using high school teachers who have participated in an intensive seminar on writing as trainers of other high school teachers. This policy avoids the problem of having high school teachers feel "dictated to" by university professors who have never themselves taught in a secondary school. At the same time, however, since college faculty members generally organize the seminars and workshops, opportunities for communication between secondary and postsecondary English teachers are built into the basic structure of the project.

Some schools approach the improvement of high school English curricula by giving secondary and postsecondary teachers firsthand experiences in each other's classes. In 1982 San Francisco State University and San Francisco's public schools established a project entitled Learning Bridge. Teams of English teachers from the university and from San Francisco's Balboa High School work on course materials for use in courses at the high school. Once they have developed and refined these materials through classroom applications, they share them with English teachers at other high schools in the area. The program also includes plans for a faculty exchange in which high school English instructors teach university courses and university instructors teach high school courses. A similar program at Illinois State University stresses the collaborative teaching of secondary and postsecondary faculty members. In this program, high school and college English instructors team-teach in each other's classes, using each other as coteachers, advisers, and assistants. The San Francisco and Illinois approaches suggest that effective collaboration depends on having teachers from different grade levels who are familiar with the educational environments prevailing at other grade levels. This familiarity, they contend, ultimately determines the utility of the assistance they can offer one another.

The University of South Dakota's Extended Teacher Institutes take a cross-disciplinary approach to developing secondary humanities curricula. Drawing on high school faculties from Iowa, Minnesota, Nebraska, and South Dakota, this program brings together teachers from different disciplines to develop multidisciplinary courses with the assistance of university faculty members. Thus, a literature teacher and a history teacher from a single high school might collaborate to develop parallel courses in which they explore a common theme through literature and through history. The themes around which teachers construct their high school courses are based on the history and culture of the Upper Great Plains regions. Participating teachers investigate how to blend their subjects during an eight-week intensive summer institute, plan their courses during the following school year, and introduce the courses the year after that. Throughout this period, the university faculty members who direct the project maintain regular contact with participating high school teachers. The special advantage of this approach is its emphasis on a horizontal as well as a vertical articulation. Not only does the curriculum for a particular class blend with the curricula of similar classes at other grade levels but it also relates to the curricula of classes in other disciplines at the same grade level.

Some cooperative programs that focus on curriculum development use high school courses to prepare students for a specific course or a sequence of courses at a college or university. The Queens English Project, for example, has cultivated a partnership between teachers at several New York City high schools and teachers at the City University of New York in order to create eleventh- and twelfth-grade writing-reading curricula that will lead directly into an initial university writing course. The program has combined seminars for the high school teachers with on-site tutors in the high school classrooms to implement writing-reading syllabi intended to bridge the gap between high school and university courses. A program of this kind is most effective when a significant percentage of the students who benefit from the changes in the high school curricula attend the cooperating university after graduation.

In some states, the board of education or a similar agency brings together teams of English teachers from all grades to develop curricular guidelines for courses at the various levels. The Illinois State Board of Education recently sponsored a program in which elementary, secondary, and postsecondary English teachers developed curricular guidelines for kindergarten to twelfth-grade courses focusing on writing instruction. The guidelines they devised were published in a series of basic skills pamphlets that were distributed to writing teachers at all grade levels throughout the state. A variation on this program can be found in Ohio, where the state's board of regents and board of education formed the Ohio Advisory Commission on Articulation between Secondary Education and Ohio Colleges to study ways to prepare high school students better for Ohio's colleges and universities. This undertaking led to the publication of a "Final Report" outlining, among other things, the abilities that high school curricula in several disciplines should develop in college-bound students. The commission then distributed pamphlets based on the recommendations of this report to high schools throughout the state. While the English portions of the Illinois and Ohio pamphlets focus on writing skills, similar pamphlets could discuss the kinds of literary experiences that students should have as they move through their years of schooling.

One of the most important functions of school-college collaborative English programs should be to create professional bonds between secondary and postsecondary teachers. The Rockefeller Commission on the Humanities recently pointed out the responsibility of professional organizations, including colleges and universities, to help secondary teachers pursue professional development. The consequences of helping teachers participate in professional activities are manifold, as the Rockefeller Commission stresses:

> Sabbaticals and summer institutes . . . can inspire teachers for the rest of their careers. A number of teachers who participated in the National Defense Education Act summer institutes and the John Hay Fellows program in the 1960s remember these experiences as a high point in their professional development, an encouragement to continue to teach well, and a source of long professional relationships. Teachers who have received national recognition report that they have more influence on school policies in general. . . .   (50)

The intellectual renewal and enrichment that teachers get from professional-development programs are too often unavailable to them through their own schools, where they may be burdened with extracurricular assignments and excessively large class sizes. Although participation in professional-development activities does not eliminate these conditions, it does provide a counterbalancing positive experience. The college faculty members who conduct the seminars report that they also feel enriched intellectually and professionally by the experience.

In the summer of 1983, the National Endowment for the Humanities initiated what may prove the most influential program dedicated to furthering the professional development of secondary teachers through summer courses taught by distinguished college professors. This program, entitled Summer Seminars for Secondary School Teachers, stresses the study of major texts in history, literature, philosophy, and religion. The seminars are offered on campuses throughout the country to teachers who have been selected from a pool of applicants. Funding for each seminar covers, among other things, stipends for the participants. A somewhat similar program is the Yale–New Haven Teachers Institute. Though not national in scope, being restricted to teachers from the New Haven school district, the institute does emphasize the intellectual renewal of these participants through seminars conducted by Yale faculty members. The program also asks teachers to develop curricular units based on the insights they have gained from their work in seminars. Thus the intellectual enrichment of teachers provides the basis for student learning.

The National Humanities Faculty (NHF) encourages the professional development of secondary teachers by bringing college and university teachers in the humanities to a participating high school to help with curriculum development. After the high school has identified its needs through consultation with a representative from the NHF, university teachers capable of helping the school meet those needs are brought in as advisers. The university faculty members work with a core group of teachers and administrators at each school, a group that takes primary responsibility for developing the project. After this group and its advisers have planned a project over the course of a school year, a subgroup attend summer workshops with teachers from core groups at other schools and attempt to refine the ideas developed during the year. Thus, teachers from each school receive professional and intellectual stimulation not only through interaction with university teachers but also through collaboration with peers in the special summer workshops.

Several colleges and universities help secondary teachers develop professionally by inviting them to campus for a year or more to work with university faculty members in a special team-teaching arrangement. Georgetown's Writing Center Associates Program gives full scholarships and stipends to a small group of high school teachers, each of whom is paired with a university professor in teaching a section of freshman English. In addition to what the high school and university teachers can teach each other about how to approach a course of this kind, they develop a strong sense of collegiality that can help revitalize both. In addition, the visiting teachers take courses at the university which also contribute substantially to their professional development. The University of Illinois sponsors the Associates in Rhetoric program, in which a select group of high school instructors teach in the freshman rhetoric program for one academic year.

The visiting teachers do not team-teach with university faculty members, but they do enroll in university graduate courses and develop a camaraderie with others in the university community. The experience enables them to return to their home schools with a stronger sense of professional identity.

Funding

Because school-college cooperative programs in writing and literature call for efforts "above and beyond the call of duty" from the secondary and postsecondary teachers and schools involved, the programs generally must rely on external funding to a significant extent. Funding requirements for articulation programs in English generally fall into two categories: (1) funds to initiate a program and (2) funds to sustain an existing program. Most programs rely on a variety of funding sources for the first of these but must often turn to the participating schools or state legislatures to keep the project going once the initial funds have been depleted. In fact, when applying to some sources for start-up funds, schools developing a cooperative project must be able to demonstrate that local support will be available once the project has established itself and achieved a degree of success. Many applicants seek the combined support of several funding sources, a policy that can both make the project more attractive to each source and help ensure adequate total funds to carry it out.

The most generous funding sources in supporting school-college cooperative projects in writing and literature have been federal agencies, specifically the National Endowment for the Humanities (NEH). The endowment has funded, through various programs, a large portion of the individual cooperative projects developed by schools and colleges throughout the country. It has also established two ongoing programs designed to involve as many teachers as possible in school-college cooperation. These are the Humanities Instruction in Elementary and Secondary Schools program and the Summer Seminars for Secondary Teachers program. The first of these actually involves several programs, two of which have been especially helpful in bridging the gap between secondary and postsecondary English instruction. The Collaborative Projects program encourages schools and colleges to devise projects to improve the quality of secondary curricula in humanities subjects. The second program, Institutes for Teachers and Administrators, enables high school teachers and administrators to study humanities texts with college professors for four weeks in the summer. Then, during the following school year, the professors help the teachers work institute material into high school classes. As noted earlier, the Summer Seminars program focuses more on the professional enrichment of teachers than it does on curricular changes. This program holds special promise because it involves a large number of teachers throughout the country and because (as of this writing) it has expanded, with additional support from the Andrew W. Mellon Foundation, from fifteen seminars in 1983 to almost sixty in 1985.

How much the NEH can continue to support programs of this kind is open to question. To what degree cuts in domestic spending programs will affect the sums available for cooperative projects remains to be seen. Add to the diminishing supply of funds the increase in the number of applicants in the last several years, and the problem involved in trying to support all worthwhile cooperative projects becomes apparent. The NEH has stressed for some years the desirability of securing funds from other sources to supplement its contributions to a project, and it may be that school-college collaborative programs will have to rely more heavily than they have in the past on gifts and matching funds as a prerequisite to federal support. Then, too, to complicate matters further, far fewer agencies support projects in the humanities than do in the sciences. The increasing number of applicants do not have many alternatives to pursue if their initial applications are turned down.

Schools and colleges also receive support for collaborative projects from state-based agencies. These agencies primarily include regional offshoots of the NEH and state boards of education. State-based humanities councils generally reflect the priorities of the NEH, and although their resources are limited, they invite opportunities to combine their resources with those of other agencies to support collaborative projects. Because the state must ultimately bear the financial burden of remedial programs, state boards of education have become increasingly responsive to programs that offer a strategy for helping students prepare more effectively for writing in college. A concern over the growth of remedial writing programs in state-supported colleges and universities in Ohio inspired the Ohio Board of Regents to provide funds for Early English Composition Assessment Programs. These programs encourage schools and colleges to work together to evaluate the writing abilities of high school students and to revise writing curricula in the schools so that graduates will be capable of college work.

Another type of funding source for school-college cooperative programs in writing and literature is the private foundation. The Rockefeller Commission on the Humanities specifically called on private foundations to support a series of "neglected areas," one of which was "programs of collaboration between schools and colleges" (179). Because the need to improve teaching and learning in secondary schools has received considerable attention in the past few years, both local and national private foundations seem more prepared to invest in collaborative projects. Two of the larger private foundations that have given substantial support to collaborative programs in English are the Ford Foundation and the Andrew W. Mellon Foundation. Since such projects are generally planned for specific communities or limited geographical regions, they are eligible for funding from smaller private foundations designed to serve local areas. Such foundations, however, draw on more limited resources and stress projects with a high publicity potential.

Those developing collaborative projects have had some success in applying to yet another type of funding source—private corporations. Again, a few corporations can be singled out for the substantial support they have given to programs of this kind. Foremost among these are the Atlantic-Richfield Corporation and the Exxon Educational Foundation. Since corporations favor projects that address clearly identifiable social and public problems, much of their support has gone toward collaborative projects aimed at developing writing skills. They tend, however, to regard quality education generally as an important public issue. So, when the Carnegie Report on Secondary Education in America states that "the quality of the American high school will be shaped in large measure by the quality" of the schools' connections to higher education, collaboration itself becomes worth funding.

Finally, if schools and colleges expect to sustain collaborative projects capable of significantly affecting the quality of secondary and postsecondary English education, they must identify internal resources that will support the projects on a long-term basis. Some programs are so structured that they need little or no outside support; yet these are in the minority. Most promising programs can secure the initial funding, but to conduct their projects permanently, they must get the cooperation of administrators at all the participating schools at the very start and give clear evidence of success. Many of the school-college programs involved in the National Writing Project have lasted beyond the initial funding period because they have done exactly this. As a condition of their participation, the schools applying for funds to initiate a project of their own were required to match the $15,000 maximum grant contributed by the NEH through the Bay Area Writing Project. This requirement both ensured the commitment of these schools to the project and created an automatic basis for funding once the initial funding period had expired. The success of the National Writing Project increases the chances that the schools will continue to commit this money to their local projects.

Problems and Recommendations

Collaborative programs depend greatly on the care invested in setting them up. They often fail either because they lack a carefully articulated agenda or because they do not use and acknowledge the contributions of everyone involved. Without a carefully articulated agenda, participants may expend a great deal of energy and never seem to accomplish anything. As a result, when they recognize that the program has not improved their circumstances, they abandon it, more convinced than ever that cooperation is a waste of time. The failure to recognize the knowledge and abilities of all participants has the same ultimate effect; teachers feel used rather than useful, and the result is greater distance between teachers at the two levels than existed before the program began.

In his national survey of school-college collaborative programs, Gene Maeroff advances five principles that should govern their operation. His recommendations suggest how those in charge of these programs can avoid the above problems.

1. School and college administrators must begin by recognizing that they have common problems, and they must base their agenda for cooperation on these problems (*School and College* 3). Working on shared problems makes high school and college administrators and teachers more prepared to invest in the program and take responsibility for its success because they see it benefiting them directly.

2. Faculties at both levels must eliminate "the traditional academic 'pecking order'" (3–4). When participants try to maintain this relationship, they increase the chances that the knowledge and abilities of all participants will not be valued, and therefore used, according to their merits.

3. School-college cooperative programs "must be sharply focused" (4). Projects should concentrate on one or two common goals. Individual participants should have the opportunity to identify what they expect the program to achieve for them and their schools. The program should then blend the selected goals into a plan of action that the teachers are capable of carrying out.

4. Participants at all levels must be rewarded for the efforts they invest in the program (4–5). The collaborative efforts of university teachers should receive the recognition accorded other professional and scholarly activities, activities they would spend their time on if they were not involved in a collaborative program. High school teachers should have the chance to gain professional recognition through publications and presentations at professional conferences. This opportunity would create a sense of professional self-esteem too often denied them. Finally, if participants must invest a great deal of extra time and effort in the program, they should receive adequate compensation. Whether released from a portion of their regular duties or given stipends, they should not be made to feel that their participation is one more item to add to a long list of other unacknowledged obligations.

5. School-college cooperative projects "must focus on action—not machinery" (5). Once administrators and teachers have agreed on a common set of goals and have devised a plan for achieving those goals, they should not let secondary issues (e.g., the logistics of collaboration or budget considerations) become important enough to undermine executing the plan. Too often, a worthwhile and promising agenda is defeated because participants become preoccupied with red tape.

The recommendations advanced in Maeroff's study can determine the success of a school-college cooperative project because they show how to avoid basic problems that can keep a cooperative project from getting very far. Other problems, however, may not threaten the success of a cooperative project but may diminish the quality of the experience it provides for everyone involved. Thus, to the above recommendations should be added five that can show administrators and faculty members how to make experience in a project as rewarding as possible for secondary and postsecondary students and teachers.

6. A persistent problem limiting the success of many cooperative programs is the inability of secondary teachers, when they return to their individual classrooms, to maintain the enthusiasm for teaching and learning that often develops through their interaction with other high school and university faculty members. To combat this problem, the Rockefeller Foundation's Commission on the Humanities recommends the implementation of long-term projects. The commission argues that long-term collaborative projects provide an ongoing support that can keep teachers from experiencing a letdown when they return to their classrooms at the end of a project (56). In fact, cooperative projects should be self-renewing. Once the projects have achieved an initial set of focused goals, teachers should articulate new goals that build on past accomplishments.

7. Colleges often fail to use effectively two of their most important instruments for communicating with high school administrators and English teachers—admission standards and teacher-training programs. This mistake is most counterproductive when the colleges go to great lengths to set up collaborative projects and then do not apply the instruments that can inform and reinforce these projects.

Scott Thompson, executive director of the National Association of Secondary School Principals, noted in a 1982 interview, "Right now, the colleges are genuine in their feelings that too many students are not adequately prepared for higher education. On the other hand, if the colleges had a modicum of conscience they would know that their own shift in standards and requirements had something to do with the situation that faces the schools today" (qtd. in Maeroff, *School and College* 9). College English departments should clearly publish and disseminate what they expect of students entering their courses, and they should integrate these expectations thoroughly into their work with high school English teachers.

The 1961 NCTE Commission on High School–College Articulation complained that inadequate teacher-training programs were in part responsible for the gap between secondary and postsecondary English education (93). This issue is as relevant today as it was twenty-five years ago. Therefore, college English departments should study their teacher-training programs to ensure a high correlation between their expectations of high school English teachers and the objectives of the courses in their own English education programs.

8. School-college cooperative programs have not done enough to demonstrate that they are solving the problems they intend to solve. In a foreword to Gene Maeroff's study of such programs, Ernest Boyer notes, "Teachers get some training, students get a chance to accelerate their education, a school and college share facilities. In few instances is there any formal documentation that the change has made an enduring difference" (ix). Collaborative projects in English should devise effective strategies for evaluating the impact of their efforts on English education in their schools. Determining the effects of an articulation program can serve two critical purposes: (a) the results can provide participating teachers with a basis for determining where and how to revise the programs and (b) positive results can provide a strong argument for continuing administrative support.

9. "High schools do not carry on their work in isolation," Ernest Boyer has noted. "They are connected to elementary and junior high schools and to higher education, to industry and businesses, to state and federal governments that provide support, and, above all, to the communities that surround them. In the end, the quality of the American high school will be shaped in large measure by the quality of these connections" (*High School* 251). School-college programs are not intended to cultivate some of these connections, but ultimately they should become the means of interconnecting all levels of education. So far, college faculty members have focused on working with high school teachers because they are most immediately affected by what happens to students in high schools. Once high school–college connections have been firmly established, however, articulation efforts should also extend into junior high schools and elementary schools. This further collaboration will increase the continuity of the English education that students receive and will enable them to learn more effectively at every educational level than they currently do.

10. Perhaps the greatest danger facing collaborative projects is the idea that they are fads that have grown out of a crisis in humanities education and that they will disappear once the crisis has passed. Murray Sachs stated the problem in a recent essay on cooperative programs in foreign language education: "As a temporary expedient of crisis management . . . the case for school-college collaborations would seem compelling. . . . And yet, there are troubling questions that need to be addressed. . . . Will the case for collaboration still be valid after the current crisis has been resolved?" (42). The answer to the question is, of course, yes. College administrators and teachers, however, should resist the tendency to consider school-college cooperation a fad. They should take

steps to institutionalize these programs, steps that might include appointing tenure-line faculty members to maintain liaisons with nearby schools.

The essays contained in this collection demonstrate how high school and college English teachers around the country have created successful cooperative programs to address the problems they share. While all the programs described here demonstrate how the principles set forth above can be put into practice, they vary widely in their strategies for implementing these principles. The variations largely result from the different priorities, resources, and philosophies that inform the programs. Collectively, the programs represent how a wide range of schools in diverse circumstances attempt to solve a common problem. They are described here for two reasons: (1) in their different ways they have been successful, and their accomplishments deserve to be widely publicized; (2) they can serve as models for other schools and colleges interested in establishing or modifying programs of their own.

Much current research in learning theory stresses the importance of the continuity of the learning process. If they accomplished nothing else, school-college collaborative programs in English would be worth the expense and effort because they are the means through which this interconnectedness can be achieved in English education. However, as the essays in this collection repeatedly demonstrate, cooperative programs can also provide the intellectual stimulation that makes teaching English intrinsically rewarding. Although articulation in English education now seems to have regained the prominence it deserves, we must not forget that for a period in the recent past it more or less got lost among the other issues preoccupying the English-teaching profession. For the sake of the quality of education in writing and literature that students receive at all grade levels and for the sake of the intellectual enrichment of English teachers at all levels, this should not be allowed to happen again.

Georgetown University: The Articulation Program and Related Projects

James F. Slevin

In 1977, in collaboration with the District of Columbia public schools, Georgetown began an effort to improve the teaching of critical reading and writing in local schools. From the fall of 1977 through the spring of 1981, English teachers from Georgetown and from all twelve of the district's public high schools worked together to consider ways of improving the teaching of composition and literature. We always assumed that we had a lot to learn from one another about teaching and that the boundaries that had prevented us from talking with one another served only to hurt our students. To overcome these obstacles, Georgetown sponsored a graduate seminar that enabled us jointly to study current rhetorical and literary theory and to discuss the application of that theory to classroom practice. During the first three years of the program, we planned each successive stage together, so that our project grew from the advice of those who knew what such a program ought to be doing—the classroom teachers themselves.

Throughout the first few years, but especially in the 1980–81 academic year, we began to consider what was missing—what we were not accomplishing and what needed to be done. This critical examination led us to apply to the National Endowment for the Humanities (NEH) for funding to achieve the goals of the new, revised program we envisioned. The endowment responded favorably to the proposal, awarding us a grant for approximately $200,000 to implement a three-year project to improve the teaching of the humanities in schools and colleges in the District of Columbia.

Problems and Revisions

The quality of our current program is directly related to the care we took to evaluate our earliest efforts, recognizing problems and arriving together at workable solutions. First, since one of our great laments during those years was that the program was limited to English teachers, we concluded that all teachers had to become concerned with student writing, not only assigning it but *teaching* it. We therefore decided to include teachers from other humanities disciplines, so that we now bring together six teachers from Georgetown and about thirty junior and senior high school teachers who represent various disciplines.

Second, in evaluating our early efforts, we considered it unfortunate that only public schools were represented in the program—as if we were acceding to the stereotyped depiction of a contest between public and private education, especially in urban areas. So, we decided to invite private schools as well as public schools into the project, to discuss both similarities and differences and to benefit from exchanging ideas about teaching.

Third, we saw that our original project, like most programs of this kind, worked with teachers without paying direct attention to the variety of situations in which they taught. In effect, we ignored—"tried to escape" might be closer to the truth—important and complicated institutional realities. So, in remaking the program, we created it not only for teachers but for schools. Our assumption is that successful teaching differs as circumstances differ and that these institutional pressures have to be taken into account. This is one reason why our program runs during the regular academic year, from September through May, and not during the summer. We can thereby involve other teachers, administrators, and students from all the participating schools. For example, we plan regular meetings with principals to explain the progress of our program and to suggest changes that might be helpful, given the particular circumstances in each school.

Fourth, we found that although we had worked hard for a whole year, we had nothing *tangible* to show for our efforts. While all of us might have become better teachers of writing, we constituted only a small fraction of the teachers in the area struggling to solve the same problems we faced. What could be done for them? We decided that participants in our program should create and publish assignments that could be shared with teachers throughout the district and, as it turns out, with educators from all parts of the country.

To summarize, then, our NEH-funded program is now characterized by four features, all of them the result of suggestions made by teachers who participated in the early years of the program:

1. We bring together teachers from many different disciplines and levels.
2. We bring together both public and private school teachers.
3. We bring together not only teachers but schools—faculty, administrators, and students.
4. We extend our work to others—in Washington and across the country—by the publication and wide dissemination of curricular materials.

Objectives

The defining purpose of our program is the cultivation of what we term *critical literacy*. By *literacy* we mean what Paulo Freire and Walter Ong mean: a critical awareness of writing as a cultural form enabling certain kinds of thought and certain kinds of action within a given community. Such a view sets itself against most current theories of literacy education, which simplify, indeed trivialize, the concept of literacy. Many administrators and teachers, faced with students needing remedial work, have often moved to a behaviorist model that narrowly defines literacy in terms of "minimum competency." They thereby offer simplistic notions of "technical training" and "survival skills," notions that presume that the student must absorb certain elementary skills *before* implementing them in acts of analysis, discovery, communication, and persuasion. In this view, education is a passive and lonely experience, not the development of talents to be shared but the isolated elimination of flaws; the learner is seen as inactive, merely receptive—and very much alone.

Against this passive and solitary view of learning, our program aims to consider the entire range of literacy education, from the teaching of basic skills to the teaching of complex literary works, difficult historical problems, sophisticated philosophical ideas—what might best be termed not basic literacy but critical or cultural literacy. It is obvious, then, that we consider literacy not simply an ability to master elementary skills, but a cultivated capacity to interpret and compose complex discourse. In such a view literacy includes a content, a knowledge of historical events and literary works and philosophical ideas worth interpreting and writing about to others. We take for granted that writing should be taught as a way of learning. What we want to examine is how learning and the exchange of what is learned occur differently within different disciplines. How can writing be used not only to help students learn but to cultivate their critical awareness of this function of writing and of the nature of the discipline itself? We therefore regard writing both as a defining feature of the *content* of the humanities (i.e., texts to be studied are *writing* as we use the word) and as a *humanistic* activity that aims to engage others in inquiring about that content.

Structure and Procedures

Operating within this conception of literacy, teachers from all levels, from junior high through graduate school, meet regularly in small workshops devoted to the content of the humanities disciplines. Each year we sponsor at least five such workshops, each coordinated, but not "taught," by a Georgetown faculty member participating in the program. Within each workshop the selection of the materials to be studied and the direction of particular meetings are shared responsibilities. The year is divided in half, with the first half (September through January) devoted to open-ended explorations of two related concerns, concerns we address on both a theoretical and a practical level.

First, the concern with teaching: What works and what does not work in the classroom? How can we most effectively organize courses, conduct classroom discussions, use small-group interactions, and so on? In particular, how is writing related to the students' thinking and learning? How can we create writing assignments that help students become interested in our subject and that relate this material to what the students know and feel about the world?

Second, the concern with the humanities themselves, a concern not just with how we teach but with what we teach—and why we teach: Why is it important that our subject matter be passed on to another generation? How can we help one another better understand the disciplines we teach and their relevance to our own lives and the lives of our students? We assume that our primary responsibility as teachers is to know what we teach. So, pursuing the truth—not just what "works"—is our central goal.

Here is just a brief illustration of how these concerns can be united. Participants in one of our literature workshops might spend a week studying poems by Robert Frost and Langston Hughes, discussing how to interpret and teach these works, particularly by giving students effective writing assignments. We confront the problems of teaching this literature. How can writing help students to see connections between Hughes's use of literary language and their own use of language, or to become aware of the different social origins of Frost's and Hughes's poetic practice? As we discuss these works and the way writing helps in teaching them, we become aware of fundamental questions about the nature, value, and centrality of writing at all educational levels.

In this respect, we found as we went along that our workshops were taking up some of the central questions raised by contemporary literary theorists—particularly reader-response criticism, semiotics, Marxist criticism, and rhetorical criticism. Once we finally freed ourselves from our first impression that the day-to-day lives of high school teachers couldn't possibly be affected by specialized theoretical inquiry, we found that just the opposite was true. These theories—especially because of the fundamental questions they pose—can contribute significantly to the teaching of literature and writing. What forms of discourse have a central, not marginal, role in the lives of students? Why do they? And what connections can be made between the writing and reading that students actually do and the complex art we have them study? One purpose of our program has been to foster cooperative consideration of such questions and of their relevance to teaching the humanities.

In the second stage of our program (February through May), we turn to the development of curricular materials for our own classes and for wider distribution. Participants submit their drafts in stages, and at each stage (from tentative proposal, through drafting, to revising and editing) they receive guidance from all the other workshop members. We serve one another as a kind of "support group," arguing interpretations, challenging assumptions, suggesting different types of assignments or teaching strategies, and so on. The result of these months of collaborative effort is *Writing in the Humanities*, a three-volume set of curricular materials published annually that can be distributed to any school system, or school, or individual teacher that wishes to use them.

As mentioned above, these volumes have received great support from educators throughout the United States, primarily because the format of our publication makes the curricular units especially useful to classroom teachers. Each unit, arranged as a sequence of reading and writing assignments, requires anywhere from three to six weeks. For each day, we offer two kinds of advice to teachers. First, we suggest classroom activities (lecturing and discussion strategies, questions to raise, problems to anticipate, and so on) and the specific goals of these activities. Second, we prepare writing assignments that can be given to students, assignments that help students explore for themselves the topics or questions discussed in class. We formulate questions to help students see the significance of the topic to their own lives, making them care about the topic by locating it within what they already know. We also carefully explain what we expect of the students, how they can meet our expectations, and how they should prepare for class the next day. Instead of giving students just the topic and the format for the paper, we try to provide detailed guidance on the process of composing (prewriting, drafting, revising, editing).

This format was developed by teachers who participated in our program during the 1980–81 academic year. They considered it a form within which they could undertake both theoretical and practical explorations of effective teaching. In offering day-by-day suggestions to teachers and students, the form is basically narrative. Into this narrative structure, we build theoretical explanations, speculations about writing and teaching, and specific suggestions for students to consider while writing and for teachers to consider while planning their classes. As narrative, the form allows us to relate inquiry, and to accommodate theory, to the temporal reality of a teacher's life.

Plans and Related Projects

The success of our NEH articulation program has encouraged Georgetown to explore other ways of establishing effective cooperation between college and precollege educators.

First, as a result of conference presentations and publications about our program, we have been contacted by school teachers or administrators from virtually every state. They have expressed strong interest in our curricular materials, and as of the summer of 1984, educators from almost a hundred schools or school systems have purchased our *Writing in the Humanities* series. We intend now to take some initiative here, rather than simply wait for schools to approach us. We will make our materials known, and available, to school systems around the country. In this way, our past and continuing efforts can reach the widest possible audience and have the greatest possible impact. We are also negotiating with a university press to publish selections from our ten volumes; we have in mind a two-volume work that uses our best materials—especially those concentrating on British and American literature. These constitute exemplary discussions of, and suggestions for, teaching literature and writing—created *by* classroom teachers *for* classroom teachers.

Second, we have instituted at Georgetown what we call the Writing Center Associates Program. We now bring to Georgetown—on full scholarship plus stipend—a number of high school teachers (usually four) seeking master's degrees in English that combine the study of composition pedagogy with the study of literature. Each associate is paired with a Georgetown professor, and together they team-teach two sections of freshman writing, sharing equal responsibility and authority for the courses. The associates are thus in direct contact with more students, for more hours, than any other teaching assistants at the university. They do the students at the university an extraordinary service, while gaining from the experience a clearer sense of how their own teaching can better prepare students for postsecondary education.

They also do wonders for Georgetown's regular faculty members, who have come to value them as colleagues who can often do a better job with freshmen than the professors can. Such an attitude helps both college and high school teachers break the barriers between them. The high school teachers seem to value this collegiality, and the experience has made them far more likely to invite Georgetown faculty members to visit their schools and talk with their administrators, thereby providing occasions for mutual enlightenment and opportunities for improving the quality of instruction and curriculum in the schools.

A third project to promote collaboration between colleges and schools is a seminar, offered every summer, on the teaching of writing in various disciplines. Each summer, ten Georgetown faculty members—five from English, five from other departments—meet with approximately thirty high school, community college, and college teachers to discuss ways of approaching writing instruction. This seminar has broad appeal, bringing together teachers from suburban as well as inner-city schools and colleges. Of the ten Georgetown professors participating each year, several are always *new* to the seminar, so that we are constantly extending and deepening the interest of our own faculty members in this kind of cooperation. Because many of those who enroll in the seminar are colleagues or professional acquaintances of previous participants, a small network is being established, which is good for our graduate program (many applications for the Writing Center Associates Program have come from this network) and even better for our continuing efforts to improve the teaching in local schools. A fourth project recently established involves a focused effort to work with teachers in local Catholic schools. Georgetown has hired a former participant in the Articulation Program, Patricia O'Connor, who offers special workshops throughout the year in a project sponsored by the local archdiocese. This sequence of workshops, which might be considered a "satellite" of the larger Articulation Program, attracts approximately thirty teachers each year.

Fifth, Georgetown has joined with other local universities and school systems to form the National Capital Area Writing Project, a site of the National Writing Project. We have hired a full-time, tenure-track assistant professor, Daniel Moshenberg, who is helping to coordinate the various activities and constituencies of the project.

Our final project, and perhaps our most significant vehicle for achieving university-school cooperation, is the publication of a journal. *Critical Literacy* is published three times a year, with each issue devoted to a specific topic of professional interest to our colleagues in local schools and colleges. Through the journal, which follows the format employed in our *Writing in the Humanities* series, we provide an additional forum in which teachers can publish their ideas about their work. Teachers who publish with us, along with those who read the journal, have begun to conceive of themselves as authors "writing" their courses (in the form of assignment sequences). Each of these sequences has a single identified author, and in each article the teacher's convictions remain central. So, for us, the development of curriculum becomes an act of authorship addressed to others in the community, specifically the community of students in our classes and the community of fellow teachers who read our publications. *Critical Literacy* thereby serves as both a resource and a symbol. As a resource, it offers practical suggestions about the craft of teaching, enables us to keep in touch with former participants in both the NEH project and our more recent cooperative programs, and encourages others with similar interests to join us. As a symbol, it represents what we are trying to do. In all our collaborative programs, teachers from different levels work together to establish literacy education within the humanistic disciplines, assuming that even the most basic literacy skills can and should be taught within regular courses in the humanities and social sciences and assuming as well that knowledge of these disciplines is an aspect of literacy. To achieve this integration, we have created a community of different disciplines and of different kinds of schools, defined by a commitment to specific goals that promote critical literacy. A journal that enables us to write to and for one another about our work symbolizes both the critical and the communal aims of our endeavors.

Recommendations: The Goals of Collaborative Programs

What the various Georgetown projects aspire to do is to encourage everyone (both teachers and students) to become what Freire calls the agents of their knowing and what, from our point of view, might be better termed the *authors* of their knowing. We do this through writing, which for us has three dimensions:

(1) writing as the texts we study, (2) writing as the activity or process that helps us study them, and (3) writing as the vehicle for an exchange that binds together a community devoted to understanding and questioning these texts. Through writing, understood in all these dimensions, we discover our role as the makers of our own knowledge and, to that extent, as the makers or authors of a culture. This active, culture-creating function of education is the very thing that many high school students and teachers have been told they cannot conveniently or efficiently achieve. Their work is the attainment of survival skills—both student *and teacher* resting content to survive in a world fashioned by others. To say the least, such a view trifles with the pain and bondage of mere "survival." Our various programs propose instead that, through writing, students can discover the critical and creative dimensions of knowing—particularly if they write extensively about the humanities and attempt to express what they know so that others will understand and accept it. And teachers, to guide such knowing, must engage themselves in writing that is similarly critical and creative—becoming the authors of the courses they teach.

We believe that this conception of literacy, by addressing itself to the most serious needs of students in the schools, serves also as the most effective preparation students can receive for college courses in the humanities. Moreover, it is not only the college-bound students who are well served but also the colleges, and in particular the humanities programs, for which the students are bound.

Humanists are more than selfishly concerned about the decline in funding and other institutional support for the humanities at universities across the country. As advanced humanities courses decrease in number and enrollment, untenured faculty members are threatened with dismissal and scholars must abandon the kind of teaching that nourishes their research. It is obvious now that we must do more than simply lament these conditions; we must act to ensure that the advanced study of the humanities remains a central part of the university's educational mission.

Much now depends on attracting students to take humanities courses and to major in humanities departments. But students will be attracted only if they come prepared to understand the benefits of humanistic study, not just the personal and professional benefits of being a humanities major among "cultural illiterates" but the intellectual benefits inherent in prolonged and intensive inquiry about the humanities. The problem here is preparation. How well are students prepared to benefit from the advanced study universities can offer them? How "critically literate" are they? Obviously, humanities courses cannot justify themselves unless we help students to examine, question, appreciate—do anything but simply ignore—that justification. In Georgetown's view, the solution to this problem involves extensive efforts to establish collaborative programs between colleges and schools. Further, these efforts cannot remain isolated endeavors; the solution requires better communication and greater cooperation among colleges and universities committed to improving American education at all levels.

Bard College: Institute for Writing and Thinking

Paul Connolly

Bard is a coeducational liberal arts college of eight hundred students, located on the Hudson River, ninety miles north of New York City. Since 1979 it has operated Simon's Rock, an "early college" of three hundred students in Great Barrington, Massachusetts, fifty miles from the Bard campus. Students typically enter Simon's Rock during the tenth or eleventh grade of high school and follow a fully accredited program of studies that leads to completion of the first two years of college at the usual age of high school graduation. They may then complete their BAs at Simon's Rock or Bard or transfer to another college. Because of the Simon's Rock–Bard union, the college has a special interest and experience in school-college cooperative programs, and it sponsors many activities—an annual January conference, a Distinguished Scientists lecture series, and an NEH-sponsored summer seminar for social studies teachers—that bring secondary and postsecondary teachers together.

Background

After experimenting for two summers with an intensive three-week workshop in language and thinking for its entering freshmen, Bard College established the Institute for Writing and Thinking in September 1982 with the aid of $600,000 in grants from the Booth Ferris, Ford, and, later, Exxon foundations. The institute provides workshops, consulting, and conferences for high school and college teachers who want to improve interactive instruction in critical reading, creative thinking, and clear writing in all courses. In the institute's first three years, fifty-three hundred teachers from several hundred high schools and colleges availed themselves of these services, enrolling in the one- to seven-day workshops held on Bard's two campuses, seeking on-site consulting, or attending conferences sponsored by the institute and other organizations.

Leon Botstein, the president of Bard, initiated the required freshman workshop in language and thinking in the summer of 1981. He appointed Peter Elbow, author of *Writing without Teachers* and *Writing with Power*, to direct the program; Elbow, in turn, hired twenty teachers, in various disciplines, from schools around the country. Each teacher worked with ten students, 5½ days each week, in three 90- and 120-minute workshops a day devoted exclusively to close, responsive reading; rich, probative thinking; and engaged, spirited writing. The following summer, Simon's Rock adapted an eight-day version of the workshop to the special needs of its entering class.

In the course of five summers, forty teachers with collective experience in over one hundred educational institutions—high school, community college, college, and research university—have conducted these workshops as an experimental laboratory that incorporates and extends the best current theory and practice of writing instruction. They teach varied subjects—English, history, philosophy, psychology, anthropology—at various grade levels; write extensively themselves; and usually play a central role in the writing programs of their home institutions. Thirty of the teachers serve not as independent experts but as associates of the institute, faithful to teaching methods tried and proved collaboratively. Cooperating on all projects and meeting two weekends a year to review and refine their work, the associates present workshops, conduct conferences, and consult with other teachers.

Objectives

All activities are experiential. Associates of the institute do not "talk at" their teaching colleagues but rather provide an opportunity, through workshops, for individuals to write and reflect together, to listen to one another, to examine their habits and expectations as teachers and writers while experimenting with alternatives to present practices. All workshops promote active, collaborative learning rather than competitive or passive schooling: a frontal assault of information transmitted, received, recycled. The institute seeks to foster in the classroom and among teachers learning communities that support risk taking and bold, adventurous learning—in the belief that such communities give students and teachers alike a sense of their own capacities and a desire to know more.

The institute defines writing—to use a phrase Seymour Papert applied to the computer—as "an object to think with" (11). It does not consider writing a "basic communication skill" learned by handbook rules and handout exercises. Writing is a more liberal art than that: a complex, imaginative act in which the mind uses language to engage the world and create meaning for itself. All institute programs demonstrate interactive instruction in reading, writing, and thinking, in the conviction that reading and writing—"construing and constructing" (Berthoff 10)—are complementary instances of the active imagination making meaning: thinking. All programs resist gimmicks, recipes, and glib talk of basic tools, examining instead the deeper, long-term question of how thought evolves through written language.

The ultimate objective of the institute is to improve students' writing by changing attitudes and assumptions as well as aptitudes. Its immediate objective, however, is to serve teachers by helping them share what they know and become better at what they do.

Programs

In its first three years, the institute conducted fourteen weekend and eight week-long workshops in teaching writing and thinking for nine hundred teachers, meeting in groups of ten or twelve, on the campuses of Bard and Simon's Rock. It presented workshops of a day or longer, focused usually on "writing across the curriculum," for another two thousand teachers at sixty-two schools and colleges. It sponsored eight conferences and presented workshops at many others. And it designed and provided various other workshops that are not so easily categorized: for first-year law students at the Benjamin Cardozo School of Law; for law professors at Washington and Lee University; for graduate management students at the New School for Social Research; for nonteaching adults at Wainwright House (Rye, NY) and at Bard; for school administrators and for teachers of poetry; and for groups of thirty high school students from fourteen schools, accompanied by their teachers, over fourteen weekends at Simon's Rock.

The institute has found that talks, keynote addresses, and panel discussions do not have the impact of experiential, "hands-on" workshops, where participants read, write, think, listen, respond, and revise, even as they appraise their habits and assumptions as teachers and writers. Workshops provide a professional retreat where teachers representing many locations and departments and varying in age, experience, and background, can come together to examine and experiment with their own writing processes and reflect on how they learn and teach. In these workshops, teachers write and think intensively about learning communities, generative and critical writing, composing processes, supportive responses to writing, revision, critical reading, writing about texts, and writing with power and authority.

Staffing

At present the institute has the following administrative staff: Paul Connolly, full-time director and professor of English at Bard; Teresa Vilardi, full-time associate director; and Judi Smith, part-time administrative assistant.

The institute is deeply indebted to the vision of Bard's president, Leon Botstein, who fully supports the program, and also to the formative influence of Peter Elbow, now director of writing programs at the State University of New York, Stony Brook. It is the institute's thirty active faculty associates, however, who "own" the institute, along with the participating teachers who modify and extend their work. One-fifth of the associates teach at Bard–Simon's Rock; one-fifth teach subjects other than English. Almost all have ten to fifteen years' teaching experience, though some are senior faculty members and others are themselves graduate students. They are secondary and postsecondary teachers who collaborate without rank or title and are committed to a teaching community that transcends the territorial imperatives of grade levels. They teach the weakest students and the strongest, adolescents and adults, from urban and rural areas, in public and private schools and colleges. They are fully responsible for the policies and programs of the institute, they are well paid and greatly appreciated, and they aspire to model among themselves the learning community they would create in the classroom. In its collective experience and generous collaboration, the faculty is the most distinctive asset of the institute.

Funding

Bard College and Simon's Rock sustain their own freshman workshops in language and thinking, and the teaching methods developed there are the bedrock of the institute's work with other teachers. Additionally, the institute uses the facilities and resources of the college, which assumes many indirect costs.

Private foundations—Booth Ferris, Ford, Exxon, and other smaller and anonymous donors—continue to support the institute, contributing to its operating costs (administrative salaries; support services; research, evaluation, and development costs) and subsidizing the participation of schools and teachers in workshops. Wherever possible, the institute asks participating schools to pay the direct costs of workshops: materials, meals, housing (if necessary), and the fees paid workshop leaders. But money from foundations allows the institute to provide "scholarships" for those who cannot pay. Were it not for these grants, the institute's combined direct and indirect costs would prohibit many schools from participating in its programs, particularly the poorer institutions that most need assistance, and so Bard's president has begun to create an endowment to provide permanent support for the institute.

Future Plans

The institute will continue its present workshops, conferences, and consulting, but it also intends to develop new programs. Given the crucial role of school administrators in successful writing programs, the institute would like to develop workshops specifically for administrators, where they can write themselves, consider renovations in their present writing programs, and exchange ideas with other administrators. The institute will also do more work in the area of "adult literacy," piloting new workshops for nonteaching adults. Recognizing a need to strengthen teaching networks among those who have attended its programs, the institute has begun to experiment with dinner meetings, followed by workshops, in the teachers' own schools, where teachers can write together, introduce colleagues to the methods of the institute, and model successful teaching strategies for one another.

In its second year, having established basic workshops entitled Teaching Writing and Thinking, the institute developed and piloted a second and third generation of workshops, Teaching Writing in the Social Sciences and Teaching Critical Inquiry, the latter designed to help students recognize and participate in a community of inquiry, read closely and respond critically to difficult texts, and attend to the full process of inquiry that culminates in carefully reasoned argument. These workshops are now offered regularly on campus and through on-site consulting, and the institute is in the process of designing new workshops on using writing in the service of math and science courses. Since its inception, the institute has encouraged the use of word-processing systems in the writing classroom and will bring its experience to teachers through further workshops. It has also edited a collection of essays in which directors describe twenty-eight innovative college writing programs: *New Methods in College Writing Programs: Theories in Practice*, to be published by the Modern Language Association in 1986. Associates are collaborating on a second book, to consist of their own essays on teaching writing and thinking. Finally, in anticipation of providing more instruction in the workplace, associates recently completed a feasibility study on how the institute might serve high school and college "stop-outs," entry-level workers and middle-level managers in large corporations, attorneys, and retired adults. The institute has also begun planning a branch on the West Coast, so that it can better serve teachers and schools in the western half of the United States.

Problems

1. Isolation. Many teachers work alone, reliant solely on their own resources, without the support of a vital learning community in which they can discuss problems openly, admit difficulties, seek counsel, and nourish wisdom. School-college cooperation assumes teacher-teacher cooperation. Without it, institutional partnerships may be forged, but a deep rethinking of education will not occur.

2. Fragmentation. English teachers can be viewed as pieceworkers on an assembly line that assigns the production of "language arts" to the elementary school, the "five-paragraph theme" to the high school, and "higher-order reasoning and research" to the college and university. The issues in school-college "articulation," then, become how to retool parts of the line where production seems to break down and how to smooth transitions between production sectors, eliminating wasteful repetition and developing a coherent, efficient curriculum. Such a meristic model of schooling, which reduces literacy education to the acquisition of a series of "academic skills," trivializes learning. It also disposes even the well-intentioned teacher to take full authority for keeping students "on task," thus unwittingly cutting them off from their own learning. The more profound problem in school-college cooperation is the reintegration of all elements of learning into an organic, natural whole, in each grade and every course.

3. Magic. What is vaguely called the "process approach" to writing is now an object of attention in many schools and colleges. This method of teaching, however, is not plugged into a school as easily as a computer, a textbook, a faculty conference day, or a guest expert. Teachers are asked to help students take ownership of and authority for their language; to do less formal lecturing; to relax their grip on error; to promote active, collaborative learning in large classes; to write with their students; to become listeners and learners themselves. Dear habits, expectations, attitudes, and assumptions are at stake here and, even with the best of intentions, are not easily or quickly changed. Nor is the educational environment, where class size, course load, and evaluation procedures enforce these habits and expectations. School-college cooperation cannot succeed by "magic"—a new trick today, another tomorrow—but depends on open, honest inquiry by all teachers, regardless of the grades they teach, into how to help students learn and teachers teach.

4. Time and money. School-college cooperation is usually considered a form of faculty development, an opportunity for teachers to stand back from their work and gain a fresh perspective on it. There is very little time in the public school year, however, for teachers to take stock of their work, as New York State's Regent's Action Plan acknowledged when it proposed that ten days be added to the school year for staff development. An aging, senior, tenured faculty is often identified as the enemy of educational reform, and more attention is given to browbeating the faculty into submission than to releasing its potential. If collaboration within and between schools is to succeed, more time and money have to be invested in supporting teachers, encouraging their personal and professional growth, and developing their talents for imaginative leadership.

Final Observations

The Institute for Writing and Thinking is, perhaps, an unusual instance of school-college cooperation, for it represents less the collaboration of one educational institution with another than it does the collaboration of a group of individual teachers with many other teachers. Institutions do, of course, provide vital support and sponsorship, but the work itself is done by teachers and for teachers. Many college teachers are condescending toward secondary teachers. Furthermore, within their own schools, secondary teachers are often treated as hired hands, not educational leaders, and their imagination and initiative are stifled. Associates at the institute work on the uncommon assumption that teachers know a lot and qualify as experts on their own students. Respecting their experience and insight, the associates collaborate with them without condescension, presumption, intimidation, or, consequently, defensiveness. Perhaps the greatest success of the institute is that it restores many participants' confidence in their own abilities as writers, teachers, and researchers and renews their respect for, and pride in, their teaching colleagues.

The institute's associates are themselves good teachers who have discovered an uncommon strength through their own collaboration. Experience has shown them that the communal wisdom of a faculty is stronger than that of its individual members, struggling alone, in competition with one another. They test everything they do among themselves before asking students or other teachers to try it. They constantly rehearse their own teaching together, for one another, so as to recognize precisely how and why some things work and others do not. Finally, they write constantly together, valuing the imaginative energy, the richness of thought, and the opportunity to be heard that such writing brings to them.

In the experience of the institute, cooperation between secondary and postsecondary teachers succeeds best when it addresses the strengths of teachers, not the weaknesses, and involves all teachers equally in the responsibility for the success of the collaboration.

Yale University: Yale–New Haven Teachers Institute

James R. Vivian

Background

As early as 1980 two national panels issued their findings on the state of student learning in the humanities and the sciences: a joint National Science Foundation–Department of Education study spoke of "a trend toward virtual scientific and technological illiteracy" (ix) and the Commission on the Humanities concluded that "a dramatic improvement in the quality of education in our elementary and secondary schools is the highest educational priority in the 1980s" (25). The commission called for curricula to teach children to read well, to write clearly, and to think critically. They also found that "the need to interrelate the humanities, social sciences, science and technology has probably never been greater than today" (6).

National problems in secondary education are no less important to Yale than to universities generally, and Yale's reasons for becoming involved in seeking solutions transcend altruism or a sense of responsibility to the New Haven community. As Yale President A. Bartlett Giamatti pointed out in an interview on the David Susskind television program on 7 December 1980, "it is profoundly in our self-interest to have coherent, well-taught, well-thought-out curricula" in our local schools and in secondary schools throughout the country. Yale acted on such a view in 1970, when the history department began the History Education Project (HEP), which assisted a number of New Haven social studies teachers in developing improved curricula for courses in American history, world area studies, and urban studies.

The success of HEP led to discussions about organizing a more ambitious and demanding program that would include additional disciplines. Teachers and administrators from the university and the schools quickly reached a consensus: the relationship between the university and the schools must be both prominent and permanent within any viable larger relationship between Yale and New Haven, and of the many ways Yale might aid New Haven none is more logical or defensible than a program that shares Yale's educational resources with the schools. Because of changing student needs, changing scholarship, and the changing objectives set by the school system and each level of government, school curricula undergo constant revision. Because of Yale's strength in the academic disciplines, all agreed that the university could most readily assist the schools by developing curricula, further preparing teachers in the subjects they teach, and helping teachers keep abreast of changes in their fields.

Our intent was not to create new resources at Yale; rather, it was to make available in a planned way our existing strength, that is, to expand and institutionalize the work of university faculty members with their colleagues in the schools. Even at this early stage, both Yale and the schools sought a course of action that might have a substantial impact. The superintendent of schools and the board of education asked that the expansion of the program begin with the addition of seminars in English, the subject in which they saw the greatest need. The objective was eventually to involve as many teachers as possible and to include a range of subjects that would span the humanities and sciences, so that the program might address the school curricula, and thus students' education, broadly. In 1978, then, the Yale–New Haven Teachers Institute was established as a joint program of Yale University and the New Haven Public Schools, designed to strengthen teaching and thereby to improve student learning in the humanities and the sciences in our community's middle and high schools.

The Program

From the outset, teachers have played a leading role in determining how Yale and the school system together can help them meet all their students' needs, not only the needs of students who later will enter college. The institute seeks to involve all teachers who state an interest in any of the seminars and who can demonstrate the relation of their institute work to courses they will teach in the coming year. The institute does not, then, involve a special group of teachers who teach a special group of students; rather, it is an intensive effort to assist teachers throughout the school system, grades 7 through 12.

Each year about eighty New Haven school teachers become fellows of the institute to work with Yale faculty members on topics the teachers themselves have identified. Many of the university's most distinguished faculty members have given talks and led seminars in the program. Seminar topics have included geology, the environment, medical imaging, Greek civilization, architecture, the arts and material culture, the American family, and a variety of topics in literature, history, and culture. The materials that the fellows write are compiled into a volume for each seminar and distributed to all New Haven teachers who might use them. Teams of seminar members promote widespread use of these materials by presenting workshops for colleagues during the school year.

Culminating with the fellows' preparation of new materials that they and other teachers will use in the coming school year, the institute's intensive program lasts 4½ months and includes talks, workshops, and seminars. The talks are intended to stimulate thinking and discussion and to point up interdisciplinary relationships in scholarship and teaching. Presenting institute guidelines for curriculum units, the workshops explore the fellows' own approaches to writing a curriculum unit and stress the audience for whom fellows are writing: other teachers. The seminars have the related and equally important purposes of increasing the fellows' background and developing new curriculum materials on the seminar subjects. As a group, fellows study the general seminar subject by discussing common readings; individually, each fellow selects a more limited aspect of the subject and researches and develops it in depth for classroom use. Each seminar must balance these complementary, but in some ways distinct, activities.

In applying to the institute, teachers describe the topics they most want to develop; Yale faculty members circulate seminar proposals related to these topics; and teachers who coordinate institute activities in the schools, after canvassing their colleagues, ultimately select which seminars will be offered. In effect, New Haven teachers determine the subject matter for the program each year. Because English is the largest department in the schools, a high proportion of teachers' requests have been for seminars on language and literature; nineteen of the forty-three seminars the institute has offered have been in this area. These seminars may be categorized as studies of a particular genre, interdisciplinary approaches to history and literature, thematic approaches to literature, and approaches to teaching writing. Teachers of languages other than English have frequently participated, and two interdisciplinary offerings were organized specifically for Spanish and bilingual-education teachers.

In an early seminar, Strategies for Teaching Literature, led by James A. Winn, the members as a group discussed a variety of literary genres, and each fellow individually researched and wrote on a particular genre. Other seminars have concentrated exclusively on a single genre. Readings in the Twentieth-Century Short Story, led by James A. Snead, considered the unique form of the short story, various styles, and questions of interpretation, especially those related to the teaching of literature. Thomas R. Whitaker twice led a seminar on drama. In his first seminar, members addressed a range of pedagogical strategies involving drama: how dramatic improvisation can increase students' motivation for studying the language arts, how it can provide a context for exploring the situations of bilingual and black students or of adolescents as a group, and how nonverbal performance can be a useful preparation for engaging a text. In a second seminar on drama, the fellows explored the implications of assuming that, even in a classroom, a play is best read as a "score for performance." They engaged a variety of plays, sampled some theater games and exercises, and shaped their group work so that it would encompass each of the curriculum units the fellows were preparing. Autobiography, a seminar led by Richard Brodhead, considered autobiography both as a literary form and as a human act. Participants looked at some distinguished examples of autobiographical writing and discussed ways in which the study of autobiography could provide the focus for a program in student writing.

Each of the genre seminars emphasized how best to introduce middle and high school students to the genre, how to relate what students would study to their own experience, and how, simultaneously, to encourage various forms of student expression. As Brodhead wrote:

> While our seminar was reading classic writings and discussing abstract questions about autobiography, our concern was always with what this study could yield for New Haven high- and middle-school students, and specifically with how it could help develop their powers of verbal expression. This concern is constantly reflected in the units, each of which uses autobiography as the basis for a program of student writing. Our idea, in making autobiography the matrix for writing assignments, is to connect the often troubled act of writing with a broad activity of communication that students are already competent at and comfortable in. But while they draw on this reservoir of existing communicational skills, the units do not promote casual or uncontrolled self-expression as an end in itself. Rather they aim to use autobiographical self-expression to make students more conscious of the nature and power of expression, as well as to promote the forms of self-discovery—that new knowledge of who we are, where we came from, what matters to us, and why—that the writing of autobiography can produce.

Institute seminars with an interdisciplinary approach have combined the studies of history, literature, and culture. Society and the Detective Novel, led by Robin W. Winks, examined the transfer of the American "Western novel" to the asphalt of the city, showing how detective and, to a lesser extent, spy fiction reveals the nation's preoccupations. Drawing on the visual arts as well as literature, An Interdisciplinary Approach to British Studies, also led by Winks, explored recent approaches to English literature in connection with recent trends and new interpretations in modern British history. The "City" in American Literature and Culture, led by Alan Trachtenberg, explored the usefulness of the category "city" or "urban" in the teaching of American cultural history. Drawing from readings in fiction, poetry, social theory, and urban history, as well as from knowledge of their students' backgrounds and needs, seminar members attempted to reconcile the detached view of the scholar with the more practical, urgent view of the citizen. Twentieth-Century American History and Literature, an early seminar, was divided into three sections, one on American domestic affairs, led by Richard W. Fox; one on foreign policy, led by Henry A. Turner; and one on the feminine experience revealed in various forms of literature, led by Cynthia E. Russett. In The Afro-American Culture of the Twentieth Century, led by Charles T. Davis, seminar members studied, comparatively, black and white literary traditions and historical accounts of the experiences of blacks and Italians in New Haven; examined origins of the black migration from the South and of the black ghetto in the Northern city; and investigated qualities in Afro-American achievement that were distinctly black—always, however, with a concern for a debt to the host American culture.

Two seminars in literature took a thematic approach. Adolescence and Narrative: Strategies for Teaching Fiction, led by Ross C. Murfin, examined ideas held by adolescent characters and the way these characters relate to, reflect, or oppose the surrounding culture. In the broadest sense, the seminar considered the relationship between adolescence and fiction: what fiction can reveal about adolescence; whether, in fact, novels with adolescent protagonists most often represent some difficult human condition other than adolescence. The Stranger in Modern Fiction: A Portrait in Black and White, led by Michael G. Cooke, considered the idea of human freedom in such contexts as family history, political and legal systems, financial need, social customs, nature, personal failure, and myth. The Oral Tradition, also led by Cooke, explored the relation between the oral tradition and the civilization in which it is developed in three literary environments: classical Greek poetry and drama, British poetry and German folktales, and black American fiction.

The institute has offered a series of four seminars on the teaching of writing. In the first of three seminars entitled Language and Writing, discussions were based largely on the members' work in progress. The seminar leader, James A. Winn, remarked, "No synthesis or consensus emerged from these sessions; indeed, many of the differences in theory and practice between the participants may now be more sharply defined and more deeply felt than they were. But I can state confidently as the seminar leader that the marks and dents of all that vigorous shoptalk are visible on every unit." The seminar the following year, led by Thomas R. Whitaker, was intended for teachers who were preparing curricula dealing with some aspect of grammar, reading, speaking, or writing. In a third seminar, again led by Winn, common readings included material on rhetoric and linguistics, and fellows were encouraged to design a curriculum unit substantially unlike anything they had done before. The fourth seminar on writing, Writing Across the Curriculum, led by Joseph W. Gordon, involved teachers from all disciplines, not only English. They investigated both current research on the composition process and teaching methods that grew out of that research, and they drew up model assignments for getting students to write more often without a proportional increase in the teacher's work. As Gordon wrote:

> The seminar out of which these units developed engaged in spirited and extended disputes that, we hope, clarified the differences among us. There are units here that regard writing as a means, and others that regard it as an end in itself. There are units that advocate the use of drills, and others that instead use poetry and art to teach syntax and vocabulary. Some units suggest using haiku, others suggest writing postcards and letters, and one even speaks of the advantages of formal outlining. Some concentrate exclusively on techniques for developing the students' self-confidence and creativity. There are units here for teaching writing in the history and science class, as well as in English and foreign language classes. And a few units address students for whom English is a second language or who are classified as Developmentally Disabled. There are, in short, strategies here for almost any student in the middle or high school. Out of all this variety, we hope, the thoughtful and energetic teacher may discover, or just rediscover, a reason and a motive for "assigning more writing."

For all fellows, whether in English or in other disciplines, working on writing and on the teaching of writing is a central purpose and activity of the institute. Almost two-thirds of them have stated that the process of writing an institute curriculum unit improved their own writing, and over three-fourths have reported that the experience improved their ability to teach writing effectively—whatever their field. To fulfill the requirements of the program, each fellow must prepare a curriculum unit of at least fifteen pages containing four elements: (1) objectives—a clear statement of what the unit seeks to achieve; (2) strategies—a unified, coherent teaching plan for those objectives; (3) classroom activities—three or more detailed examples of teaching methods or lesson plans; and (4) resources—three annotated lists: a bibliography for teachers, a reading list for students, and a list of materials for classroom use. The discussion of objectives and strategies must be in prose and must constitute at least two-thirds of the completed unit.

What fellows write, then, is not "curriculum" in the usual sense. They are not developing content and skill objectives for each course and each grade level, nor are they preparing day-by-day lesson plans for their courses. Institute units also differ from traditional curricula in form; they are not composed mainly of outlines of topics to be covered. Instead, teachers research and discuss in writing some aspect of the seminar subject that they will use in their own teaching.

Fellows develop their curriculum units in six stages, each a month apart. Initially, in applying to the institute, teachers describe the topic they wish to develop and its relation to school courses. At the second meeting of the seminar, each fellow, having consulted with the seminar leader and other seminar members, presents a refined statement of his or her topic and a list of basic readings for research. Each then writes, based on preliminary research, a two- to four-page prospectus that describes what the final unit will contain and that provides all seminar members with an overview of their colleagues' work. The next stage is the first draft of the statement of each unit's objectives and strategies, which is distributed and discussed in the seminars. A second draft includes the revised statement of the objectives and strategies of the unit and a first draft of the unit's other elements. The completed unit is due about three weeks after the seminar's final meeting. At each stage, fellows receive written comments from the seminar leader as well as responses from other teachers in the seminar, a part of the audience for whom fellows are writing.

The institute, in short, regards the preparation of curriculum units as a process, and this concept is widely understood and accepted by the fellows. One participant wrote that "the process provided a comfortable format, a logical progression of reading, thinking, and writing." A veteran fellow wrote:

> After five years' experience, I find the process for unit writing a very balanced, flowing process. The more experienced a unit writer I become, the more convinced I am of the necessity and wisdom of the stages of the writing process. The prospectus gives the Fellow the momentum to move from the reading to the writing stage, although it does not necessarily curtail the continued research; the first and second drafts give the author an opportunity to refine his presentation.

From a university faculty member's point of view, Brodhead wrote:

> The system of repeated drafts for the curriculum units was especially important in my seminar: I was very rigorous in my evaluation of the early drafts, and I was insistent that Fellows work at strengthening and clarifying what was weak and vague in those drafts; and I'd have to say that they without exception faced the challenges I set them, and moved, draft by draft, toward a much more significant, and much more fully-articulated, proposal. Touchingly, many of them said that it had been years since anyone took their work seriously enough to criticize it; in any case, the way they use the seminar leader's comments as a means to a fuller grasp of their own thinking was enormously impressive to me.

The Institute's Governing Principles

Four principles, all implanted in the first institute in 1978, and each shaped over time by experience, guide the program and constitute much of its distinctiveness. They are (1) our belief in the fundamental importance of the classroom teacher and of teacher-developed materials for effective learning; 2) our insistence that teachers of students at different levels interact as colleagues, addressing the common problems of teaching their disciplines; (3) our conviction that any effort to improve teaching must be teacher-centered and our consequent dependence on the institute coordinators, teachers in each school who meet weekly with the director and who constitute an essential part of the program's leadership; and (4) our certainty that the university can assist in improving the public schools only if we make a significant and long-term commitment to do so.

The institute differs from conventional modes of curricular development. Classroom teachers, who best know their students' needs, work with Yale faculty members, who are leading scholars in their fields. The institute does not develop curricula on certain topics only because these topics are important in recent scholarship; rather, it brings knowledge to the assistance of teachers in areas they identify as their main concerns. The institute involves no "curriculum experts" in the usual sense, who would themselves develop new materials, train teachers in short-term workshops to use these materials, and then expect the materials to improve classroom teaching. Instead, the institute seeks to demonstrate that intensive and long-term collaboration between a university and its neighboring school system—between schoolteachers and university scholars—can produce curriculum materials of high quality that pertain to student needs and can significantly influence teaching and learning in the schools.

By writing a curriculum unit, teachers think formally about the ways in which what they are learning can be applied in their own teaching; we emphasize that the institute experience must have direct bearing on their own classes. In the end, their units reflect both the direction provided by the Yale faculty members and their own experience in the classroom, their sense of what will work for students.

This balance between academic preparation and practical classroom application—as well as the depth and duration of our local collaborative relationship—are the central features of the Yale–New Haven Teachers Institute. Our outside evaluator in 1980, Robert Kellogg, pointed out:

> That Yale does not have a school or department of Education is in this instance a blessing. Without an intermediary buffer, softening, exaggerating, or explaining away the contrast of intellectual milieu between secondary education and higher education, the two groups of teachers (the Institute Fellows and the Yale faculty) are free to explore for themselves the extent to which they share values and assumptions about their subject and its role in the development of children's minds and characters.

The institute is the only interschool and interdisciplinary forum enabling schoolteachers to work with one another and with Yale faculty members. In referring to the collegial spirit of the program, we are speaking of a dynamic process that brings together individuals who teach very different students at different levels of their subjects and who bring to the program a variety of perspectives and strongly held points of view. The tensions and disagreements that arise from these different perspectives are a source of vitality and innovation. Each challenges the preconceptions of the other, with the result that university faculty members understand something more about teaching at the secondary level while schoolteachers often reconsider their expectations of their students' ability to learn. With our emphasis on the authority of the secondary school teacher, the bond between fellows and Yale faculty members is one of mutual respect and a shared commitment to the best education for New Haven students.

The institute is organized to foster this sense of collegiality. Fellows are not students paying tuition for regular graduate-level courses. Instead, they are remunerated, each fellow receiving an honorarium on successful completion of the program. As full members of the Yale community, fellows are listed in the university directory of faculty and staff; this symbolizes our recognition of them as colleagues and has the practical value of making Yale resources readily accessible to them. Through the institute, teachers gain access to human and physical resources throughout the university, not only to those specifically organized by the institute.

Also contributing to the collegiality is the informal, flexible style of the seminars—a tradition established by the first group of Yale faculty members who taught in the program and maintained by some continuity of faculty and by faculty meetings with the coordinators and the director. This makes the institute utterly unlike the graduate-level courses in education most of the fellows have taken and often unlike the graduate seminars most of the Yale faculty members ordinarily teach.

To practice collegiality in the day-to-day workings of the institute, we devised an administrative structure that would reflect the primacy of teachers. We did not wish the program to be something concocted by Yale and imposed on the fellows, nor did we wish to create different classes of fellows by involving New Haven school administrators in administrative roles in the institute. At the most practical level, to avoid placing the Yale faculty members in authoritarian roles, we hoped to use peers to solve problems of absence or lateness. The coordinators have provided a solution to all these potential difficulties. Again, Kellogg's report puts the matter well:

> In order that the "managerial" aspect of the school administration not be reflected in the operation of the Institute, a small group of teachers, the Institute Coordinators, serves to "represent" both the schools in the Institute and the Institute in the schools. The conception is ingenious, and the individuals who serve as Coordinators are, more than any other single element, crucial to the Institute's successful operation. The Coordinators I met were thoughtful and intelligent men and women who understood the purpose of the Institute and were effective representatives of the two institutions of which they were members.

Through the coordinators, who collectively represent every middle and high school teacher in the humanities and in the sciences, teachers are directly involved in the cyclical planning, conduct, evaluation, and refinement of the program. Through them we have developed and maintained both rigorous expectations and an accommodating schedule, so that there has been a high level of participation by New Haven teachers. Between 1978 and 1983 forty percent of the New Haven secondary school teachers in the humanities and the sciences successfully completed at least one year of the institute. The participants' evaluation of the program confirms the crucial role of the coordinators; one fellow wrote, "as long as there are teacher Coordinators, the program will belong to all the participants." This proprietary feeling of teachers toward the institute, the feeling that it is "teacher-centered," is essential to our success.

To participate in so demanding a program, teachers must believe that the institute can assist them in their own teaching and that, by extension, it can eventually improve teaching and learning throughout the schools. Our evaluator in 1981, Ernest L. Boyer, wrote in his report:

> The project has teacher-coordinators in each participating school who clearly are committed and who pass on their enthusiasm to colleagues. One of the most impressive features of my visit was the after school session I had with these Coordinators from the New Haven schools. Arriving after a fatiguing day, the teachers turned, with enthusiasm, to key issues. How can the Institute best help us meet our goals? How can we improve our work? . . . The dedication and optimism of these teachers was impressive, almost touching. . . . The significance of teacher leadership cannot be overstated.

Using common sense, we know that the impact of the institute will be roughly proportional to the number of teachers who participate on a recurring basis. The institute's influence on teachers' preparation and curricula is cumulative; we must annually involve a large enough proportion of New Haven teachers to be credible in claiming that their participation can improve the public schools. Each curriculum unit a teacher writes represents only a fraction of all he or she teaches, and the very nature of the academic disciplines and their teaching is not static but constantly changing. Should the institute ever become so limited in scope or duration as to appear trivial, it would cease to attract a sizable percentage of New Haven teachers and would become ineffectual. In one of its principal recommendations the Commission on the Humanities concluded:

> Because schools change slowly, we endorse models of school-college collaboration that emphasize long-term cooperation. We recommend that more colleges or universities and school districts adopt such programs for their mutual benefit, and that funding sources sustain programs and administrative costs on a continuing basis. Programs of school-college collaboration offer the best opportunity to strengthen instruction in the schools while providing intellectual renewal for teachers.
>
> (56)

As our evaluator last year, Theodore R. Sizer, noted, "Such renewal does not come quickly. It benefits from sustained contact, from supportive conditions, from simmering." It is therefore most encouraging that, after five years of developing the Teachers Institute as a model of university-school collaboration, Yale decided to seek a $4 million endowment to give the program a secure future.

Yale and New Haven together have supported a major share of the total cost of the Teachers Institute. A considerable portion of our remaining need has been met through strong and continuing support from the National Endowment for the Humanities. We have been pleased also to receive operating funds from numerous foundations and corporations—including more than fifty local businesses that see our efforts to improve the education of all young people in the area as a good form of community development. The present endowment campaign underscores our deep belief in the long-term significance of the Teachers Institute for the university and for our community's public schools. It also represents our determination to demonstrate that effective collaborative programs can be not only developed but sustained.

Recommendations

There is, in my view, no more important recommendation in the Carnegie Foundation *Special Report on School and College* than the one—contained also in the Carnegie report *High School*—that calls for universities and schools to develop genuine partnerships based on the needs of schools as determined by their principals and teachers. Both aspects of that recommendation are essential: not only that universities and schools work together but especially that those of us in higher education encourage our colleagues in the schools to show us the ways we can marshal our resources to address their needs.

I would offer the following guidelines for the successful implementation of the Carnegie recommendation:

1. *Collaboration* is a term currently used to describe quite varied activities. I mean by the term something specific. Collaboration arises from a recognition of mutual interest between school and college—between city and college—that must become more widespread if we are to improve our public schools. To be authentic, a partnership should be a coequal relationship of colleagues, a volunteer association of individuals who choose to work together, of allies in league to improve our schools. Equal importance must be attached to what each partner brings to the relationship. The aim is to have teachers work together without having to change places.

2. Because institutional and other resources are never adequate, an early step in establishing a collaborative program is to assess the resources that can be made available to meet the needs of schools and then to apply these resources in an intensive way where the need is greatest. Institutional support must come from both sides of the partnership; tangible and visible evidence of such commitment is essential.

3. We especially need to encourage partnerships between schools and universities that concentrate on teaching and on the continuing engagement of teachers with their fields. Cooperative efforts should insist on a direct application in school classrooms.

4. A tendency in establishing collaborative programs—indeed in school reform efforts generally—is to be too ambitious. Programs will succeed only if they have well-defined and manageable goals; they should avoid making impossible claims.

5. Precisely because each collaborative project can achieve only limited, though important, results, participants must be confident that their efforts are worthwhile. An ongoing evaluation process is therefore integral to a program's design and should be used perennially to refine both goals and activities. Because collaborative programs are often seen, unfortunately, as nontraditional—because they may not be regarded as central to the mission of either partner—they have a special burden of providing good evidence of their results.

6. The most successful projects may well begin small, investing real authority in teacher leadership and developing organically according to the needs teachers identify. In that way, programs are not guided by preconceptions but grow from their own local experience. Efforts at school improvement will not succeed without teacher leadership. In this country we have for too long held teachers responsible for the condition of our schools without giving them responsibility—empowering them—to improve our schools.

7. For all the above reasons and—I cannot overemphasize this point—for the benefits to be lasting, collaborative programs must be long-term.

Not all teachers are sanguine about the prospects for public secondary education. But the vision of our institute, which many share, is that the problems confronting us are not intractable and that teachers, working through the institute, can improve the education and the lives of their students. By assigning greater prestige and power to schoolteachers and by engaging them in study and writing about their disciplines, the Teachers Institute implicitly questions whether teaching in school and teaching in college should be regarded as markedly different. The educational levels and institutions in this country are not discrete and separable compartments but parts of a whole educational process, for teacher and student alike. Continuing study and writing about a subject benefit schoolteachers no less than their university colleagues. In both cases, their students are the ultimate beneficiaries.

Note

Portions of this essay are based on material in *Teaching in America: The Common Ground*, rev. ed., New York: College Board, 1984. Copyright © 1983 and 1984 by James R. Vivian.

Queens College, CUNY: The Queens English Project

Donald McQuade and Sandra Schor

The Queens English Project (QEP) is a collaborative program designed to create a "bridge curriculum" in writing and reading between Queens College and selected "feeder" high schools in New York City's Queens County. Our purpose has been to improve the writing skills of college-bound high school students during their junior and senior years of secondary school and their freshman year in college. We have sought to develop a group of students who would enter college intensively trained in reading and writing skills and who might risk taking college courses that demand sophistication in these skills, courses that for several years have shown declining enrollments at Queens College. In the six years since it was first funded by the Fund for the Improvement of Post-Secondary Education (FIPSE), the Queens English Project has benefited from the support of virtually every constituency in secondary and higher education: college faculty members, chairpersons, and administrators; high school teachers, chairpersons, principals, district and city-wide supervisors; graduate student instructors; graduate and undergraduate tutors, as well as high school and college students.[1] And more than twelve years after the first conversations that led to its development, the Queens English Project remains a workable testament to the principles and results of spirited, professional collaboration.

Background

Queens College of the City University of New York is a commuter school. Most students who enroll as freshmen have attended one of ten feeder high schools. In examining the scores these students received on the English Placement Test, and later on the CUNY Writing Assessment Test, we found that between forty and sixty percent of our entering students placed in the prefreshman writing course and that a substantial number were so deficient in their reading as to disable them in courses demanding careful and heavy reading. Our colleagues in the high schools supported this view and wanted to improve their students' training.

 The Queens English Project had its genesis in two prior projects: Common Concerns of English Educators and CUNY's Open Admissions Program. In 1973, while meeting with a member of the college's secondary education department as part of the routine task of supervising student teachers, a high school English department chairperson asked why so many honors high school English students were placed in the basic, prefreshman English course. This simple question eventually led to a series of meetings with high school English chairpersons and college English and secondary education faculty members. Those early meetings were intense. The high school chairpersons were convinced that the college faculty members would blame them for failing to teach high school students to read and write effectively. The college faculty members, in turn, anxiously tried to avoid being blamed for maintaining unrealistic standards for incoming freshmen. Gradually, the joint efforts of the group (formalized in 1974 by a calendar of monthly meetings and called Common Concerns of English Educators) bore fruit. The results are best exemplified by an agenda of topics important to all teachers of English (e.g., "Exactly what do we mean when we say we teach English?") and a collaborative leadership, with a high school chairperson and a college faculty member as cochairs. After several years of meeting, talking, and establishing mutual respect and professional trust, we decided to figure out how we might both extend our collaboration to teachers and implement some of the innovative ideas we wanted to test out in our classrooms. We realized that we needed financial help. We spent nearly a full year exploring and discussing a grant to expand our work, but we had trouble getting beyond the talking stage during that year.

Meanwhile, we had been working for more than six years with open admissions students at Queens College, directing our energies toward improving the chances of these basic readers and writers for success at our college. We experimented with teaching techniques; we read the available literature; we wrote articles; we developed special courses. One of these special courses designed for incoming freshmen was first offered in the summer of 1975. Thirty-two students who scored extremely low on our writing-reading placement tests were invited to participate in a program intended to improve their writing and reading skills so that they might begin the fall semester in English 110, the first of our required two-semester freshman sequence, instead of English 105, our prefreshman course. Students in that program wrote and read intensively every day. Tutors were available nine hours a week for individual tutoring. Class time was given over wholeheartedly to a carefully sequenced curriculum in writing and reading, and these activities proliferated. Student attendance during this six-week summer session was nearly perfect; student responses to the program were uniformly enthusiastic.

Finally, in December 1976, several Queens College faculty members attended a meeting of Networks, another FIPSE project, in Washington. At this conference, speech after speech and workshop after workshop reminded us that underpreparedness was to be expected of college-bound students. We considered carefully the ways that underpreparedness had become institutionalized, and we resolved to design a project in collaboration with our feeder high schools that would combine what we had learned through the Common Concerns and Open Admissions projects about teaching writing and reading. The convergence of these interests and components led us to apply to FIPSE for funding.

Objectives

We proposed to collaborate initially with the English departments of five representative "feeder" high schools—Beach Channel, Flushing, Grover Cleveland, John Adams, and John Bowne—to "deinstitutionalize" remediation at the college level and to demonstrate the educational, social, and financial benefits of a productive professional relationship between a college and the secondary schools whose graduates constitute a sizable percentage of its annual enrollment. We aimed to develop an English curriculum that would span the third and fourth years of secondary school and the courses in which a student acquired the basic skills now required for graduation from college. We recognized that such a curriculum might well be replicated at other colleges and schools to produce similar results: increases in student proficiency in writing and reading, appreciable gains in student sensitivity to the lifelong pleasures of these particular skills and to the humanistic disciplines in general, brighter student prospects for participating in the verbal dimensions of American experience, and, with all this, a corresponding reinvigoration of faculty morale.

Graduates of the five cooperating high schools constitute a cross-section of students entering the college each year: most come from lower- and middle-class working families; many are first-generation college students. And it has been our experience that most were generally neither very active nor energetic readers and writers. The Queens English Project set out to change these attitudes by developing a detailed sequence of interrelated curriculum models for teaching writing and reading more effectively throughout the "bridge" years of high school and college.

After numerous conversations, the founding QEP participants agreed on the following specific objectives for our collective work:

1. To reduce the number of students from the "feeder" high schools who would be required to complete so-called remedial courses before enrolling in Queens College's two-semester sequence of required composition (a decline that would decrease the cost of remediation to the college and increase the college's retention rate)

2. To return to the secondary schools the concentrated activities of readying students to do college-level work

3. To minimize the personal "costs" of remediation (by making students more familiar with the discipline and pleasures of writing and reading in their high school classes and less likely to suffer from the anxieties, embarrassments, and incapacities that attend a lack of preparation for college courses)

4. To use reliable information to build realistic expectations for student performance in both basic and elective courses

5. To help students acquire the skills that will enable them to enjoy the rewards of more challenging elective courses

6. To enable students to develop a greater sensitivity to the many ways language can serve various personal and professional interests

7. To reverse the decline in faculty morale, occasioned by a lack of confidence in teaching writing and reading to underprepared students

8. To have college faculty members work productively with their colleagues in the secondary schools to expand their collective knowledge of how, what, when, and where students learn to read and write, as well as to identify and implement the abilities needed to teach these enabling activities

9. To formulate a curriculum considerate of student accomplishment rather than error

10. To articulate the rationale and to coordinate the instructional techniques and curricular materials that lead to more successful and replicable teaching and learning

11. To institutionalize articulation between the college and the secondary schools, thereby creating a more spirited community of intellectual inquiry in which professional collaboration can flourish.

Structure and Procedures

These are the main activities through which we pursued our objectives.

Teacher Seminars

A significant outcome of the QEP was institutionalizing high school–college articulation at both administrative and instructional levels. We accomplished this double articulation through carefully planned collaborative seminars, whose participants included administrators and teachers from the high schools as well as the college: chairs of high school English departments, participating high school English teachers, directors of the Queens College Writing Program and the Academic Skills and Resource Center, teachers of college courses in the required freshman composition sequence, and doctoral candidates at the Graduate Center, CUNY, who were engaged to establish a writing-reading laboratory in each of the participating high schools. Our seminars tested and adjusted the model curriculum developed by the grant committee; it was therefore essential that they include those who would have a primary connection with students in both the high schools and the college.

Members of the seminars were always active participants rather than observers. Participants entered a process that engaged them in a sequence of reading-writing activities that included, among other exercises, free writing, writing and rewriting whole structures (such as sentences, fables, and academic essays), responding to the writing of peers and students, discovering syntax, and observing "live" classrooms. In summary, participants in the seminars focused on the whole piece of writing as well as on its abstract and concrete elements. They read published and student writing to elicit ideas about student writing as literature, responded to writing by making observations and inferences, and repeated the few activities central to developing skill as a reader and writer. They also practiced a friendly interchange about skills and attitudes with colleagues who taught students at higher and lower levels; created daily strategies and assignments for a learning-centered classroom; erased arbitrary distinctions between high school English and freshman composition, turning eleventh- and twelfth-grade English and freshman composition at Queens College into a continuing sequence; and devised valuable connections between teaching writing and teaching reading and grammar.

Department chairs, teachers, laboratory supervisors, and members of the grant committee attended the seminars for one year. As new schools joined the project, new seminars were organized. By consistently requiring the attendance of chairpersons as central figures in the unfolding seminar dramas, we produced a cadre of trained administrators who could be counted on to do two things: induce change in other members of their staffs and influence principals to designate a portion of their budgets to the continuation of the project after external support for the project came to an end.

Seminars were held weekly at the college in the late afternoon, after the end of the high school day. During federal funding, all participants (except the members of the grant committee) were paid stipends for attending; after federal funding, the stipends were discontinued.

Tutors attended a separate training seminar led by a member of the grant committee.

Articulated Curricula

The grant committee devised a provisional curriculum based on Marie Ponsot's syllabus for basic writing and adapted to the particularities of a school's circumstances by its participating teachers. The curriculum teaches reading and writing through whole structures, that is, units of discourse, complete in themselves, that instruct or delight readers. The curriculum reduces drill work and other exercises that tend to fragment reading and writing into isolated and meaningless skills. Through prolific reading and writing, the curriculum aims to teach students to read and write habitually and competently. Reading textbooks and writing exposition are a significant, though not an early, feature of the curriculum. We found it inefficient to separate the teaching of reading from the teaching of writing; we found it efficient to teach both subjects through the identification of abstract and concrete elements in whole structures with such impressive forms as riddles, fables, aphorisms, parables, and anecdotes. After mastering these structures, the students applied them in writing essays, proposing ideas (often abstract) and supporting them with concrete examples, anecdotes, comparative analyses, and so on. Our use of these concepts was strengthened by the influence of ideas discovered in the work of Josephine Miles, Northrop Frye, and Leo Rockas.

The collaborative seminar, then, became a place to identify recognizable written structures and to develop day-to-day strategies with which to teach these structures to students. Some of the principles underlying these pedagogic strategies should be noted:

- Writing extends and develops thought.
- Reading is inseparable from writing.
- Continuing practice strengthens the learner.
- Writers identify what has been done well by the responses of their peers.
- Comments on what is read aloud take the form of observations; writers revise according to the inferences they draw from the collected observations.

These principles were arrived at in the seminar inductively only after the group had worked together as a writing-reading class. Participating teachers then adjusted the syllabi to the needs of high school and college students.

Laboratories in the High Schools

Principals and chairpersons in the high schools committed themselves to arrangements of space, scheduling, and staff assignments to accommodate a writing-reading laboratory in each participating school. Laboratories were staffed by college-trained tutors—undergraduate and graduate students at Queens College who were supervised, during the years of FIPSE funding, by doctoral candidates studying at the Graduate Center, CUNY. After funding had ended, the services of doctoral student supervisors were discontinued, and each high school supported a reduced class load for one of its own teachers to supervise its laboratory and coordinate tutoring. Because individual attention is a crucial aid to mastering writing-reading skills, especially among those served normally by large, impersonal institutions, our curriculum integrated weekly small-group or one-on-one tutoring for every student as a regular feature of the project.

The way undergraduate and graduate tutors worked varied from one high school to another. The chief patterns of instruction follow, with some schools combining two or more of these practices:

1. Two to four tutors participated in every QEP classroom, working with classroom teachers to help carry out the syllabus, lead small groups, and respond to student writing. Small groups enabled every student to read his or her own writing at every class meeting and get responses from four or five peers, in addition to a tutor, and allowed every student to present an immediate observation—usually in written form—on the essay or literary work under class discussion.

2. The English class was frequently divided into halves, one-half remaining in the classroom with the teacher, the other attending the lab with tutors. Through carefully prepared syllabi and day-to-day collaboration between tutors and teachers (usually practiced on the fly in school corridors), both groups covered identical work, with students alternating from lab to classroom each week.

3. A laboratory was put into place in a convenient, attractive location in each participating high school. Supervised by doctoral candidates, the labs were staffed by tutors. Students in QEP classes arrived by appointment before or after the school day or for scheduled visits during class time, having been excused on a regular weekly schedule from their English classes to meet with tutors in the lab.

4. The laboratory was open to any high school student—not only those in designated QEP classes—having difficulty learning to read and write effectively. In some schools students learning English as a second language came to the lab for help.

Wherever possible, we attempted to place laboratory tutors who were graduates of our participating high schools in their "home" schools. Thus they often had the advantage of firsthand knowledge of the unique circumstances of that school, its students and faculty. The collegiality of such tutors presented high school students with a live and highly accessible model: a college student often just a few years older than they and from their own neighborhood interested in reading and writing and who exhibited the rewards of these activities.

Tutors were trained in the curriculum and in the decorum of collaborating with high school teachers. They were paid approximately the minimum hourly wage for time spent tutoring, traveling to and from the schools, and attending training sessions. Graduate students received a small supplement.

Chief among those who benefited from the participation of tutors and doctoral fellows in the high schools were the tutors and fellows themselves. Asked to evaluate their experiences in the Queens English Project, many wrote that the project profoundly altered the way they thought about writing, the teaching of writing, and the acts of mind involved in learning.

Staffing

College faculty members. Six college faculty members wrote the proposal for the QEP, obtained FIPSE funding, designed the project, and administered it. They formed the grant committee, under the coordination of a director and codirector. They were Janet Brown, director of testing and research (secondary education dept.); Judith Fishman, director of the Writing Skills Workshop (English dept.); Betsy Kaufman, director of the Academic Skills and Resource Center (Secondary Education dept.) and now dean of students; and Donald McQuade, Marie Ponsot, and Sandra Schor, all of the English department. Each received a reduced teaching or administrative load to allow time for his or her QEP duties. The committee was assisted by a part-time administrative assistant.

CUNY doctoral fellows. During the first two years of funding, a doctoral fellow—a candidate for the PhD in English at the Graduate Center—was appointed to establish and supervise a writing-reading laboratory in each of the five participating high schools. All doctoral fellows participated in the teacher seminars.

Undergraduate and graduate tutors. Undergraduate and graduate students at Queens College were screened, trained in the QEP curriculum, and placed as tutors in the high schools according to the needs of students in a particular school (see "Laboratories in the High Schools," above).

High school chairpersons. The project required that the chairperson of the English department in each participating high school become an active member of the teaching seminar, doing all writing and reading assignments, responding to the work of peers, and devising strategies for instruction.

High school teachers. The number of teachers participating in each high school varied from one to eight. With five participating high schools, the total number of teachers in a given year ranged from twelve to sixteen. All were experienced writing teachers; all volunteered to learn a new curriculum geared to strengthening the writing and reading skills of students; all participated in the teaching seminars. During the first two years of funding, each participating chairperson, teacher, and doctoral fellow received a stipend. Attendance at the seminars was excellent. Teachers wrote the syllabi that were finally put into use in their classrooms.

High school and college administrators. The QEP committee made a point of arranging frequent lunches, conferences, and evaluation sessions attended by the superintendent of high schools in the borough of Queens, principals of participating high schools, the provost and assistant provost of the college, the chair of the college English department, chairs of high school English departments, and members of the grant committee. The climate of collegiality that these regular occasions created between the high schools and the college finally broke down many of the barriers that had separated them and upset the hierarchical biases that have always existed between secondary and postsecondary institutions. They discovered that they had the same students, separated by a few months in age or overlapping in age, and that educators at the two levels were in fact counterparts of each other. The growing successes of the project in the schools and its national prominence through FIPSE soon became a shared pride among the various regional administrators, who looked with respect on this important example of articulation between urban institutions.

Funding

Federal funding. In 1978–80 the QEP operated under an award totaling $218,293 from the Fund for the Improvement of Post-Secondary Education: in 1978–79, $98,293; 1979–80, $120,000. Disbursements were chiefly for the following: the salary of a part-time administrative assistant; adjunct replacements for the six college members of the grant committee; stipends for high school chairpersons, teachers, and doctoral candidates to participate in the teacher seminars; hourly wages for undergraduate and graduate tutors, covering tutoring, training, and travel time to and from the high schools; testing and evaluation materials; and joint conferences on the progress of the project in the schools for high school and college administrators.

Post-FIPSE funding. After federal funding ended, the Queens English Project became institutionalized under local support. From 1980 to 1984 the project continued in the schools under collaborative funding by the New York City Board of Education and Board of Higher Education.

In the first two years, the superintendent of high schools in the borough of Queens budgeted approximately $10,000 per year for tutors to continue their work in the schools. At the same time the superintendent authorized an expenditure of another $20,000 per year to apply and extend the syllabus and principles of the project to a writing-across-the-curriculum program in Queens. The Board of Higher Education, through the office of the provost at Queens College, absorbed the cost of a reduced load for one college faculty member to continue as director of the project.

From 1982 to 1984 the superintendent no longer provided funding from the central budget. Each participating school had to support the continuation of the project out of its own discretionary funds. Three high school principals (two former participants and one new one) agreed to undertake this responsibility and budgeted somewhat less than $10,000 to pay for tutors in their schools. The college continued to support the cost of a college-based QEP director, paying a $10,000 adjunct salary for part-time duties. Local funding provided no stipends for attendance at teacher seminars.

Problems and Prospects

With the withdrawal of stipends for teachers and chairpersons who attended the seminars, attendance fell off sharply, and within a short time the teacher seminars disbanded. Undergraduate and graduate tutors continued to be trained in the principles of the QEP by the project director, but the absence of a teacher-development program dissipated their contribution, rendering their work in the schools a general tutorial service. Tutors were asked to strengthen the skills of students whose teachers had no training in the QEP curriculum.

In 1982, however, the Teacher Center program of the United Federation of Teachers invited a member of the original grant committee to give an in-service course based on QEP principles. That course has been offered each semester since, though attendees have chiefly been elementary and junior high school teachers.

A conference for teachers of writing, conducted under QEP sponsorship and held in April 1984, attracted teachers from all levels; a permanent committee has been organized to continue the discussion of QEP principles in later conferences and workshops. In addition, the QEP syllabus has become central to English instruction in the new demonstration school of Queens College, Townsend Harris High School; teachers there receive training through a special seminar conducted by faculty members experienced in the project. More recently, one of the directors of the QEP has taught the undergraduate methods course in English in the secondary education department at Queens College. Faculty members regularly assigned to that course have taught a section of freshman composition instead.

Several years beyond federal funding, then, the Queens English Project continues to help develop more fluent writers and readers in the secondary schools—and in the elementary and junior high schools—of New York City and in several adjacent suburban school districts. From all accounts the principles of the project still help nourish the professional lives of the teachers who took the risks necessary to ensure its success. But from this now fairly distant perspective, we can better view—and perhaps evaluate—the problems that still nag us and the potential that still excites us.

All of us who participated in the Queens English Project thought we knew—going in—how complex a project we had designed. But none of us could ever have imagined how much time we would spend on the administrative and pedagogical details that continually affect literally hundreds of people—many of whom face quite different anxieties and fears in each phase of the project's work. We would strongly recommend as a fundamental requirement for designing—or replicating—any program as complex as this one that the schedule allow sufficient time for administrative change and pedagogic adaptation. The institutional change we have encouraged simply took longer to prepare for—and effect—than we had anticipated.

Large collaborative programs like the Queens English Project, which necessarily contain many strands, require shared funding. Each actively interested institution and professional agency must underscore its endorsement by providing enough funds for faculty released time to permit the training, implementation, support structure, evaluation, and research indispensable to produce lasting change in the high schools and colleges. Appropriate stipends to ensure professional treatment of all participants are fundamental to the project's success. The QEP was fortunate in this respect during the time of federal funding. When funding ended, local monies only partially supported our work. Despite our efforts from the outset to secure continued funding, the program was substantially altered by the reduced support. In addition, our faculty participants overestimated what they thought they could accomplish with the released time available to them. The project succeeded because of the unusual professional and personal commitments and sacrifices of those who participated in it.

Yet for all its success, the Queens English Project remains a testament to the stark reality that programs are, finally, people. Convinced that the project had been institutionalized, its success ensured, many of the project's architects—in both the secondary schools and the college—gradually began to explore other professional interests. The complex web spun by our mutual interests and collaborative efforts has frayed at least at the edges, if not at the center. The problem is nothing that more money alone could fix. What the project needs now is a rededicated collaborative effort to redefine—and energize—its goals and procedures. And a truly collaborative enterprise is the best reassurance that such an effort is both practicable and desirable. In such a guilt-free, nonhierarchical professional environment, the questions we as high school and college teachers respectfully ask each other and ourselves will change as we discover what it is that we know and what it is that we now need to ask.

For a copy of the final report of the Queens English Project, readers are referred to the Fund for the Improvement of Post-Secondary Education, Grant Number G007804605.

Note

[1] The Queens English Project has been a collective professional enterprise. We would like to acknowledge the presence of all our colleagues' work in this essay, and in particular that of Janet Brown, Judith Fishman, Betsy Kaufman, and Marie Ponsot. The project's success has depended on the continued support of our founding group of teachers and administrators: Louis Accera, Melinda Altman, Shirley Budhos, Robert Byrd, Saul Cohen, George Cohn, James Costaris, Eunice Danto, Jean Edison, Beverly Fenig, Carl Field, Eleanor Friedman, Robert Fullilove, Milton Gordon, Virginia Gray, William Hamovitch, Eileen Hudson, Lois Hughson, Jack Jacobson, Jay Kaplan, Myron Liebrader, Mitchell Levenberg, Aaron Maloff, Maureen McFeely, Neddy McMills, Esther Meisell, Stephanie Medina, Richard Mikita, Saul Novack, Patricia Owen, Eileen Petruzillo, Nathaniel Quinones, Robert Rappaport, Charles Roemer, Raymond Schaevitz, Sarajean Sherk, Nathaniel Siegel, Willard Smith, Madeline Staffenell, Marvin Taylor, Steven Tribus, Philip Vitali, Paula Weil, and Dominick Yezzo, as well as the many talented undergraduate tutors who helped make writing pleasurable for many high school students.

University of California, Berkeley: The Bay Area Writing Project and the National Writing Project

James Gray

The National Writing Project (NWP) is an expanding network of collaborative school-university programs to improve writing and the teaching of writing in classrooms in this country and overseas. The NWP network now numbers 143 currently active sites in forty-five states and six foreign countries (Canada, England, Australia, Sweden, Finland, and Norway), as well as in United States Independent Schools and Defense Department Schools overseas (Europe, Asia, and Central America).

Background and Assumptions

The Bay Area Writing Project (BAWP), the parent site of the National Writing Project, was established on the University of California, Berkeley, campus in 1973–74 to attack a particular problem. Under the Master Plan for Higher Education in California, University of California campuses draw their freshmen from the top eighth of high school graduating classes, and in 1973 well over forty percent of the students admitted to Berkeley were required to take subject A, the university's pre-English 1A composition course. The proportion was initially thought to be as high as fifty percent, and *Time* reported this news to the nation in what I believe was the first of the various "Why Johnny Can't Write" stories that have been reappearing in the nation's press ever since. The writing problem was real enough at Berkeley in 1973, but it was a problem that had been around for a long time. The university began examining the writing of students applying for admission at Berkeley as early as 1898, and in 1936 it recorded the highest percentage of students ever held for the subject A requirement.

It was in the early 1970s, though, that the problem of student writing abilities began to receive serious national attention. By that time, there was also an emerging body of knowledge about writing and the teaching of writing, knowledge from research, from writers themselves, and from teaching practice. While we were beginning to know more about writing and the teaching of writing than we had ever known before, most teachers—working as they do in the isolation of their own classrooms—were uninformed about what was happening in their field, and in 1973 there was no systematic way of informing them. Furthermore, most teachers defined their field as literary studies and paid little attention to writing as a discipline.

As we began to plan the Bay Area Writing Project, we could assume that most teachers—no matter what grade level they taught—had not been adequately trained to teach writing. In a country that seemingly prides itself on a strong

3R tradition, writing had been neglected for reasons that are still difficult to identify. Elementary teachers were trained to teach reading, and secondary teachers, if they happened to have been English majors, were well read in the history and interpretation of British and American literature. In the early workshops the project sponsored in the schools, we asked teachers, "What course or what university program taught you to teach writing?" We seldom received a response to that question. But we knew that some teachers, out of their own interest in writing, had developed successful approaches to writing and the teaching of writing once they were on the job.

We hoped to bring these successful teachers together in an invitational summer institute and train them to teach other teachers in the workshops the project would conduct in the schools. But we wanted to plan right and avoid what we regarded, through hindsight, as the major flaws of past university efforts at school reform. In the late 1960s, for example, the National Defence Education Act (NDEA) Institutes brought outstanding teachers to university campuses throughout the nation for intensive course work—the sort of undertaking that universities can carry out very well. The problem with this approach to school reform is the mischief that occurs when knowledge of a discipline is confused with, or considered the same as, knowledge about how to teach that discipline. Although the teachers who attended the NDEA institutes were pleased with the programs offered, the knowledge about teaching that the participants brought with them, carefully screened as they were, was seldom tapped. Also, the NDEA institutes had no follow-up programs for the participants once the summer programs were over and no plans for having the participants work with other teachers in their own or other districts during the school year ahead.

We wanted, then, to create a new model for the 1970s, a model that would tap the expertise of outstanding teachers, a model that would train an ever-increasing corps of informed teachers—scholars who could not only continue working together over time but also conduct staff-development workshops for other teachers.

The Bay Area Writing Project was deliberately planned as a collaborative school-university effort to address a problem that was common to both levels of instruction. By recognizing the value of successful teachers, throughout a student's education, we designed a model that would make it possible for university and community college faculty members and elementary and secondary school teachers to work together as colleagues and partners. Administrators and faculty members from the university and the schools participated in the planning effort. From the start, the project was staffed and administered by school teachers, as well as by UC faculty members, with teachers released from their districts serving as full-time codirectors. Financial support also came from both levels, with the university paying the costs of campus programs and the schools paying the costs of school-site programs during the school year. These steps were major advances, but in wanting to do things right, we needed to resolve a number of other serious staff-development problems.

In the early 1970s teachers, particularly in the secondary schools, had grown cynical about the staff-development programs they were forced to attend, mandated programs that were frequently conducted by outside consultants who had never taught in school classrooms. Our programs in the schools, then, would be voluntary, open to any teacher who wished to attend. We were concerned also about the randomness of so many in-service efforts in the schools and the total lack of any sustained focus on content. We would not only focus on writing but offer a series of sessions over ten weeks or more, not single-shot, isolated workshops. We were further opposed to the universities' exclusive emphasis on secondary schools, a characteristic of most NDEA institutes. We knew that any effort to improve writing had to involve the elementary schools and, because the writing abilities of students who had completed freshman English had been declining over the years, had to involve the university and community colleges as well. But there were raised eyebrows when we indicated we would be inviting teachers from *all* levels of instruction to our institute. College and university teachers, we were told, would not participate in a program that would have them working alongside elementary and secondary teachers. If we could get them to attend, they would insist on dominating the program, and elementary teachers simply would be overwhelmed and intimidated in the same room with secondary and college teachers. Our instincts told us otherwise. Teachers who could demonstrate the successful results of sound practice at any level would be respected by other teachers. And we were counting on the natural interest of all teachers in discovering what can happen with student writing at the different grade levels when the subject is well taught.

Before we held our first summer institute, we had spent almost two full years in discussion and planning, anticipating whatever we could, resolving past problems so that they would not be repeated, and considering, to the best of our abilities, every possible matter dealing with writing, the teaching of writing, staff development, and the profession of teaching that we needed to address. We believed it was important to make the project a staff-development program, not a curriculum program as such. We were scornful of the movement toward "teacher-proof" curriculum packets and materials, but in 1972 and 1973 we did not believe we knew enough about the teaching of writing even to consider writing *the* Bay Area Writing Project model curriculum. Instead, we wanted to plan a project that would always be "open" to whatever was working in the classrooms of successful teachers. By having teachers demonstrate specific lessons and specific approaches they had found effective in their teaching, we would be identifying knowledge about writing that came from classroom-tested practice. When we asked teachers to conduct trial-run workshops for each other during the summer institute, it was as if we were casting a net to see what we could catch. The ideas and the approaches to writing that surfaced were discussed, and in time there was a growing consensus about which ones were valuable enough to pass on to other teachers in the staff-development workshops we would conduct in the schools. But at all times we would remain "open" to whatever approach produced quality student writing. The "open" nature of the BAWP model continues, and it is one of the great strengths of the project.

Because BAWP is a writing project, we thought it would be a good idea to ask teachers attending the summer institute, successful as they were at teaching writing, to do a bit of writing themselves. It seemed an obvious idea that teachers of writing should experience, once again, what it was that they were asking of their students; we would, therefore, build writing into all our programs, summer and school-year. We did not realize at that time how powerful this idea was to become. Many teachers were tentative—even intimidated by the prospect of having to write and present their writing to other writing teachers.

Some had difficulty writing pieces similar to those they had expected of their students. They discovered, once again, that revision was a matter not merely of correcting errors but usually of reworking whole pieces or whole sections of pieces. By participating in model peer-response groups, they discovered what it would take to make similar groups work in their own classrooms. And they discovered that they could do it, that they could write, and they had the satisfaction of knowing that their writing had pleased a critical audience of fellow teachers.

One final note on background. Teachers have traditionally sat in the lowest position on the totem pole of authority in matters of educational policy. Because we believed that the key agent to any educational change was the classroom teacher, we wanted to enlarge the professional roles and responsibilities of teachers in any way we could. Teaching is a profession, and we recognized teacher authority in that profession. We invited the teachers to come to the summer institute as fellows of the University of California, Berkeley. They would leave the institute as teacher-consultant *staff members* of the University of California, Berkeley, Bay Area Writing Project. In the following school year, teachers conducted project-sponsored workshops in school districts in the surrounding area, where formerly they would have sat in the audience. Teachers began to plan district staff-development programs and write proposals to fund those programs. They started writing curriculum monographs, many of which the project has published, and conducting research studies in their own classrooms. Over time, the Bay Area Writing Project and the other sites of the National Writing Project have identified and trained teachers who have received statewide and national recognition, and many have been appointed to key committees and commissions, where they are acknowledged as professional experts.

Much of the preceding discussion can be summarized in a list of the basic assumptions underlying the BAWP model:

1. The universities and the schools must work together as partners in cooperative-collaborative effort to solve the writing problem; the "top-down" tradition of past school-university programs is no longer acceptable as a staff-development model.

2. Successful teachers of writing can be identified, brought together during university summer institutes, and trained to teach other teachers in follow-up programs in the schools.

3. Teachers themselves are the best teachers of other teachers; practicing classroom teachers have a credibility—a believability—no outside consultant can match.

4. The summer institute must involve teachers from all levels of instruction, elementary school through university; student writing—if it is to be improved—needs constant attention from the early primary grades on through the university.

5. The summer institutes must involve teachers from across the disciplines; writing is as fundamental to learning in science, in mathematics, in history as it is in English and the language arts.

6. Teachers of writing must write themselves; teachers must continue to experience what it is they are asking their students to do when they ask them to write; the process of writing can be understood best by engaging in that process firsthand.

7. Real change in classroom practice happens over time; effective staff-development programs are ongoing and systematic, programs that make it possible for teachers to come together regularly throughout their careers to test and evaluate the best practices of other teachers.

8. What is known about the teaching of writing comes not only from research but from the practice of those who teach writing.

Structure and Procedures: The BAWP Model and Program Design

The Invitational Summer Institute

The summer institute (5 weeks, 4 days a week, 9:00 a.m. to 4:00 p.m.) focuses on three closely related activities: demonstration by teachers of their most successful classroom practices, study of current theory and research in the teaching of composition, and practice in writing in a variety of forms—personal, literary, persuasive, expository. The aims of the institute are simple: to provide teachers with a setting in which they can share classroom successes, to make teachers more conscious of the grounds of their own teaching and to help them broaden those grounds, to give teachers an opportunity to commit themselves intensely and reflectively to writing, and finally to identify and train a corps of master classroom teachers who can effectively teach other teachers the techniques and processes of teaching writing. After completion of the summer institutes, these trained teacher-consultants meet periodically as a group to renew and extend the advances of the summer and to conduct year-long staff-development workshops on the teaching of writing, meeting with other teachers in school settings to share their specific approaches to writing.

1. Identification and selection of summer fellows. The summer institute is invitational. Teachers participate in the program as summer fellows of the university, receiving stipends of $500 to cover the costs of tuition, books, and incidental expenses. The selection process begins with an annual call for nominations, from past participants, school administrators, department chairpersons, and college faculty members. Those nominated, approximately sixty to eighty each year, receive application forms to complete, and thirty-five to forty-five teachers are interviewed for the twenty slots open to new participants. Five additional slots are reserved for former summer fellows. As much as possible we attempt to achieve balance across grade levels—elementary, junior high, senior high, college, and university. We also seek to identify strong teachers of English as a Second Language (ESL) and teachers who have been using writing successfully in teaching disciplines other than English—science, mathematics, and social studies. The importance of this selection process cannot be overstated. We are trying to identify not only teachers who have had success with writing in their own classrooms but also those who can be equally effective as teachers of other teachers. While the success of our project does confirm our basic assumption that teachers do indeed make the best teachers of other teachers, not all strong classroom teachers prove equally strong as teachers of other teachers. During the days of the summer institute, some teachers will be recognized immediately as valuable future teacher-consultants, while others will be seen as potentially valuable given additional practice and experience (experience we can provide during monthly Saturday meetings throughout the year). Some teachers may never be used in workshops but may serve the project in other ways—for example, as coordinators of school-site programs, as writers and editors, or as teacher-researchers. The project's future depends on the continued success of its various programs, and these programs are all conducted by the teacher-consultants judged the most effective.

2. *Spring meeting.* Two to three weeks before the summer institute, teachers selected as summer fellows are invited to a planning meeting and luncheon at the university Faculty Club. This is the first occasion the participants have to meet one another, and it is in part a social event. But it is also a time to handle a number of administrative matters and, most important, to set the tone for the institute. We describe the writing assignment for the summer, so that the teachers will have the first drafts of their first papers on the first day of the institute, and we review what is expected in the demonstration workshops they will all be giving. Former summer fellows, invited as guests on this occasion, describe their own experiences during the summer institute, their feelings about what it was like to write and read their own writing to other teachers, their feelings about teaching other teachers, and their suggestions about what characterizes a good teaching demonstration. This spring meeting establishes, almost immediately, a strong group identity among the participants. They are pleased to have been invited to participate, they recognize that they will be working with a corps of outstanding teachers, and they leave impatient for the summer program to begin.

3. *Teacher demonstrations.* We usually schedule two presentations in each 3½-hour morning session, leaving some time for discussion, a discussion of the workshop itself as well as the ideas it generated. Before giving these "trial-run" workshops, the participants meet with a project staff member to talk through what they will be presenting. They are asked to focus on one idea, one approach to writing that they have found successful, and to comment briefly on why they teach writing this way and where this approach fits into the context of their teaching. Usually the best demonstrations will involve the whole group, either with a writing task or with the examination of student papers that demonstrate the effectiveness of the teacher's approach. The teachers giving these initial workshops come from classrooms throughout the Bay Area, from inner-city elementary and secondary schools, from suburban and rural schools, from local community colleges, private schools and colleges, and from the university's English, education, and subject A departments. In the course of the summer, the range of possibilities for the teaching of writing to all students at all levels is both demonstrated and discussed, and with five weeks spent participating in one another's teaching demonstrations, the summer fellows begin to develop a sure sense of what it will take to conduct a successful BAWP workshop in the schools the following year.

4. *Writing and editing-response groups.* The summer fellows write and revise five major papers during the institute and work with these papers in small editing-response groups three afternoons each week, from 1:30 to 4:00. The first assignment, covering the first four papers, asks the teachers to identify some subject they have wanted to write about and to treat that subject in four different ways, either by changing the point of view or the form or by moving from experience to idea. The teachers are free to choose their own topics, but no two

pieces are to be of the same type. The fifth assignment asks the teachers to write either a position paper (a "This I Believe" statement exploring a general approach to writing or the rationale behind a particular lesson) or a draft of a proposed school writing-policy statement that can be shared with colleagues in the fall. The Bay Area Writing Project is urging local school faculties to develop and adopt such policy positions on writing and the uses of writing in their schools. The position papers and policy statements are reproduced so that all participants can receive copies on the last day of the institute.

During the first day of the institute, teachers are divided into five-member mixed-grade-level response groups that will remain together throughout the summer. Teachers come to the sessions with copies of their first drafts for the other members of the group, who follow along silently as the writer reads the paper aloud. After this reading, the writer frequently starts the discussion. At times the group wants the paper, or sections of the paper, read a second time. Some teachers will aggressively seek a response to, or help with, their papers. "Does this work?" "Is this image effective?" "How can I say this better?" Others will sit back and leave all response to the group. These groups are at once supportive and critical, and we work for that balance. They are directed by the five former fellows who are participating in their second summer institute. All teachers submit up to six pages of their best writing by the close of the fourth week. A committee of teachers then prepares an anthology of the summer fellows' writing, frequently with line-drawing illustrations and photographs of the group members, that the BAWP office reproduces for distribution on the last day of the institute. On this last day—and at random times during the full five weeks—teachers are invited to read what they have written to the total group.

5. *Research seminars.* Starting with the first morning session of the institute and continuing through the program, there is an ongoing discussion of the relation between theory and practice. Even though the focus during these morning sessions is on identifying exemplary classroom practice, the teachers explaining their methods will often refer to key works they have read and, on occasion, to research findings that support their approaches. On Wednesday afternoons, however, we schedule a seminar that focuses directly on research. The summer fellows receive large loose-leaf binders that include selected key readings arranged thematically for discussion. The first week's seminar is typically an overview of research on writing development and instruction, with subsequent seminars on such topics as language and learning, the writing process, response to student writing, and the writing of basic writers and nonnative speakers. But these research seminars serve another purpose. By introducing the fellows to the growing body of research studies by teachers, they encourage participants to attempt studies of their own. The teachers learn about possible research methodologies, they read studies written by past summer fellows, generate their own questions for research, and prepare tentative drafts of proposals. During the following school year, teachers interested in pursuing their research questions will confer regularly with the BAWP staff.

School-Year Program

As the major follow-up activity to the summer institute, BAWP conducts a series of ten three-hour workshops on the teaching of writing at individual school and district sites. Over the years the number of invitations the project has received to offer this workshop series has steadily increased; in 1984–85, BAWP conducted fifty-eight such programs. BAWP charges $3,000 for a full ten-session series and $1,500 for five sessions, for schools and districts unable to pay the full fee. Each program is coordinated by an experienced BAWP teacher-consultant to address specific district needs. The coordinator, who has the major responsibility for the success of the series and frequently reshapes the program as it develops over the year, introduces the BAWP teacher-consultants who will be conducting the workshops, seeks responses from the audience of teachers on their successes or failures in working with the ideas that have been presented, responds to the learning logs that teachers write during the course of the program, and administers the end-of-sessions and end-of-series evaluations. The coordinator's key role continues to be further defined each year as we learn more and more about how to conduct successful programs in the schools. Because we schedule each workshop for a full three hours, the teacher-consultants have the time necessary to demonstrate their teaching strategies and to engage the teachers in discussion of the approaches and the underlying reasoning. And, most important, they have time to have the audience of teachers write about the ideas presented and to respond to one another's writing.

Besides this basic series of ten workshops, BAWP now conducts an advanced series for schools wishing to continue and to extend their ties to the program and a writing-across-the-curriculum series for either whole school faculties or individual departments. These workshops are scheduled after school hours, typically from 3:00 to 6:00, and teacher attendance is voluntary by design.

The Bay Area Writing Project now offers an extended range of programs, in addition to the basic school-site workshops, that serve approximately two thousand teachers annually.

- *Monthly Saturday meetings.* This program of morning workshops is open to all teachers who have previously participated in any BAWP program.

- *The open program.* This noninvitational, five-week summer program is modeled on the summer institute and is open to all teachers who wish to attend.

- *The BAWP-subject A program.* A summer program with school-year follow-up for teachers of college-bound students, this endeavor is addressed to teachers at major feeder schools to the Berkeley campus.

- *The BAWP preservice program.* In this graduate program for students seeking a California Secondary Credential, the student-teachers participate in a winter institute modeled on the invitational summer institute.

- *Extension programs.* The credit courses that make up this phase of the project are offered through the University of California Education Extension and are taught by BAWP teacher-consultants.

- *Writing assessment programs.* This service program trains elementary through college faculties in the procedures of holistic writing assessment.

- *BAWP-NWP publication program.* BAWP publishes works of four types—curriculum monographs, research studies, occasional papers, and the National Writing Project Writing Teachers at Work series.

Staffing and Administration

Because the Bay Area Writing Project administers not only its own local program but also serves as the lead administrative agency for the 19-site California Writing Project and the 143-site National Writing Project, its staff size—3 full-time professionals, 1 part-time editor, the equivalent of 3½ full-time clerical assistants—is not typical of other National Writing Project sites. Most NWP directors, who are professors of either English or English education, receive some released time from their regular duties, with secretarial help provided as needed. The costs of mailing, telephone, photocopying, and other expense items are usually covered by their departments or by the central campus administration. All NWP sites have leading classroom teachers who serve as codirectors. Most sites work with advisory committees of teachers and administrators, and many site directors delegate much of the administrative work to their corps of teacher-consultants. The Bay Area Writing Project has an appointed council of teachers, representing each grade level and each summer institute, that meets monthly as a forum to discuss program policy and to plan its own agenda. The council is responsible for preparing the monthly *BAWP Newsletter* and planning the monthly BAWP Saturday meetings. Over the years, it has also prepared handbooks for BAWP workshop presenters and coordinators, published an anthology of BAWP teacher writing, and evaluated the long-term effects of the summer institute on past participants.

Development of the National Writing Project

Within the first year, the Bay Area Writing Project began receiving considerable attention in the national press. As the "literacy crisis" stories began to appear in 1974 and 1975, it was identified as one of the few university programs already in place and dealing with the problem. University faculty and school representatives from around the state and nation began visiting the project with an eye to setting up something similar in their own regions, and during those early years BAWP helped establish the Duke-Durham County Writing Project and a similar project in Oregon. In 1976, when BAWP applied to the National Endowment for the Humanities (NEH) for a grant, the endowment staff and those who had reviewed our proposal saw the project as exemplary and recognized its potential interest nationwide. Shortly after we received this NEH grant, the endowment invited us to submit an amendment for additional funds to help other universities establish new writing project sites on the Berkeley model. With that amendment we established both the California and the National Writing projects. In California, with additional support from the California State Department of Education, we provided initial funding to eight new sites located on University of California and California State University campuses. With the remaining NEH funds we helped support new sites outside California—in Colorado, New Jersey, and New York—so that by the summer of 1977 there were fourteen NWP sites. Because the Bay Area Writing Project was planned, deliberately, as a local project to serve teachers within its own geographic area, the National Writing Project was planned as a federation of regionally autonomous sites that would be bound together into a network through a common commitment to the BAWP program design and staff-development model and through contractual agreements with the project. Funding from the NEH has continued, and the current grant, supplemented this year by additional grants from the Andrew W. Mellon Foundation and the Atlantic Richfield Foundation, runs through 1987. With these funds, the Bay Area Writing Project supports approved new-site applications with up to $15,000 in matching funds against an equal or larger amount raised locally by the new writing project site, a funding formula that requires strong local support and thus accounts, in large part, for the stability of the project over the years. In time, as more and more sites were developed, the statewide networks of sites in California, Virginia, North Carolina, and Alaska as well as the single site in Hawaii began to receive direct state support for their continued maintenance, either from their state departments of education or from their state legislatures. BAWP continues to support, as funds are available, individual NWP sites not yet funded directly through their states.

The NWP network now trains approximately seventy thousand teachers annually, kindergarten through university, in summer and school-year programs. Site directors meet twice a year at the annual conventions of the National Council of Teachers of English and the Conference on College Composition and Communication, and a three-day retreat is held annually at Wildacres in North Carolina. The National Writing Project network is administered by the BAWP staff and by ten site directors who serve on the NWP Advisory Board, with Don Gallehr, director of the Northern Virginia Writing Project, serving as codirector of the national project. BAWP publishes the *NWP Network Newsletter* and the NWP Teachers at Work series, written by teachers from several NWP sites.

Problems and Plans

The National Writing Project has been fortunate in having received continued support from its major funding agencies, the National Endowment for the Humanities and the Carnegie Corporation of New York, and in identifying new sources of funding through the Andrew W. Mellon Foundation and the Atlantic Richfield Foundation. At the same time, the funding level has always been insufficient to the need. BAWP can support only a third of the inquiries it receives each year from interested, potential sites; and the funds available for established sites in need, for necessary networking activities, and for lead-agency administration are far short of the funds needed. The National Writing Project and the individual writing project sites suffer the same problems that plague all university-based service programs that rely in large part on extramural funding.

The National Writing Project is now seeking additional state, federal, and private support as a national resource for excellence in American education in order to accomplish the following major goals: (1) to expand the National Writing Project into a network of 250 sites so that teachers and students in all fifty states and in all regions of the country can be served by a local writing project site; (2) to support all established sites not yet permanently supported by state or local funds and to continue that support until permanent funding is secured; (3) to test new evaluation designs to assess the effect of the National Writing Project on student writing performance, the teaching of writing, and school writing policies; (4) to expand National Writing Project programs; national and regional networking, follow-up planning meetings for new and established sites, the publications and teacher research programs, writing-across-the-curriculum and school writing assessment projects, and target projects to serve specific student populations.

Recommendations

The Bay Area Writing Project offers a tested model to universities and colleges interested in establishing cooperative programs with the schools. It is a model that has already been widely replicated—in writing (143-site National Writing Project); in literature (the literature institute at the University of Nebraska, modeled on the Nebraska Writing Project); and in mathematics (the statewide California Mathematics Project). And it is a model that has been evaluated as effective, not only in the important test of the marketplace but also in a series of controlled studies on teacher and student impact (32 of these studies are summarized in the recently published *NWP Evaluation Portfolio*). If there is any single key that would account for the project's success and stability, it is to be found in the project's basic assumptions, which have remained unchanged over the eleven-year history of the project. My major recommendation to university faculty members interested in planning a cooperative program with the schools would be to give those assumptions careful consideration.

The following five points are central in planning any effective school-university program. First, the idea of partnership must be believed. It is not a label but an operating principle. School and university teachers, as colleagues, work together to determine program policy and plan program activities. A leading classroom teacher, respected by other teachers in the area, is appointed codirector and given major administrative and program responsibilities. The cooperating schools and school districts in the area share a portion of the costs of the program. Second, there must be early and mutual recognition of the knowledge that teachers at both levels can contribute to the program, and both worlds of knowledge must be tapped. Third, if special summer institutes are planned, they must be planned to include follow-up programs that maintain the working ties already established with the summer participants and make it possible for the summer participants to share their knowledge with other teachers. Fourth, any workshops that the program sponsors in the schools must be offered as voluntary programs. Even when schools contribute released time for such programs there should be some possibility of choice offered to teachers. Last and most important, the school-university cooperative programs must be planned as success models that put a premium on what is working rather than as deficit models that treat classroom teachers as diseased, damaged, and needing repair. The Bay Area Writing Project has worked because it celebrates good teachers and good teaching.

For further information about the Bay Area Writing Project, the California Writing Project, and the National Writing Project, write James Gray, Director, Dept. of Education, Univ. of California, Berkeley, CA 94720.

Miami University (Ohio): The Ohio Writing Project–Early English Composition Assessment Program

Mary Fuller and Max Morenberg

Like National Writing Project (NWP) sites in general, the Ohio Writing Project–Ohio Board of Regents' Early English Composition Assessment Program (OWP-EECAP) is designed to retrain both elementary and secondary teachers of composition. The retraining takes place in two contexts: (1) a four-week summer institute at Miami University, in which teachers earn six semester hours of graduate credit; and (2) in-service programs conducted in local school districts, in which teachers may earn continuing-education units. In addition to retraining teachers, OWP-EECAP eases the articulation of high school students into the university through a testing, evaluation, and consulting component that calls for close cooperation with school districts. Funding for the program has come from private, university, and governmental sources.

The Retraining Program

The heart of the retraining program is the summer institute, which we run for the most part within National Writing Project guidelines. Teachers have time in the mornings to write and to share their writing within small editing groups. Teachers also read and discuss books and articles on composition theory and research, ranging from Piagetian views on cognitive development to research findings on error analysis in basic writing. Though we try not to advocate any one viewpoint, most of the readings fit within what Maxine Hairston has labeled the "emerging paradigm" (85). They cover strategies for invention and discovery; they include rhetorically based concerns like audience, purpose, and occasion; they are informed by disciplines such as cognitive psychology and linguistics. Thus most teachers leave with more process orientation than they entered with.

The teachers are also, we think, better writers by the end of the institute. They have written and discussed their writing formally and informally for well over a hundred hours. Once or twice a week we replace peer-group sharing with large-group workshops. The papers to be considered, usually one or two, are submitted in advance, copied, and distributed for "class" discussion. The workshops, which we lead, afford teachers an opportunity to share their writing anonymously with an audience beyond their immediate peer group of four or five teachers. They give us the chance to practice teacher modeling, to show how we might go about revising the writing. We can ask the hard questions a peer group often does not ask, or we—along with other workshop participants—can offer a different perspective. Thus, the teachers leave the institute not only as more practiced writers but also as more sensitive, better evaluators of writing.

Besides writing, reading, and editing, the summer institute includes presentations by the teachers themselves. Each of them must give an hour presentation on one classroom technique that has worked for them. After all, a central assumption of the writing project is that there is power in numbers. Twenty-five teachers who have solved twenty-five separate problems disseminate among the group twenty-five shared solutions. In the past, we have had teachers give presentations on vastly different topics. One fourth-grade teacher shows how to acquaint elementary students with others' physical disabilities through writing. A high school Latin teacher presents ways to apply Ciceronian rhetoric to the high school writing class. A young teacher from rural Ohio presents ways to involve students in community-based writing projects, while another teacher, from a Cleveland suburb, runs a workshop on handling the paper load. Many of the presentations are concerned with invention strategies—how to get students writing. Presenters are encouraged to involve the group in writing activities, a task they often undertake through some form of free-writing activity. At the end of the institute, the teachers write up their presentations, and we collect the papers and publish them in a volume that we distribute to teachers and administrators around the state. We have also, when funds have allowed, taken over an edition of the Ohio Council of Teachers of English journal, *English Language Arts Bulletin*, in order to publish the best papers from the institute. We think it important that teachers become published writers. Quite a few, in fact, have gone on from the institute to publish in academic outlets like the *English Journal*, the *Arizona English Bulletin*, and *Language Arts* as well as state and local journals. Even more have published in trade magazines, community and town publications, and area newspapers.

The summer institute feeds into the in-service component, which is the primary means of disseminating information and of effecting changes in the way writing is taught in the schools. We invite the most effective presenters to practice their presentations and to hone them for our in-service program. In this way, we have built up a cadre of thirty-five or forty teacher-presenters since 1980 with presentations on a variety of subjects, including the writing process, revising, sentence combining, developing a writing sequence, and evaluating writing. Schools and districts contract for these presentations individually or in series. Through the in-service component, the Ohio Writing Project has reached about fifty-five hundred teachers in over thirty districts throughout the state.

It takes a great deal of money to run a writing project, at least $30,000 per year, with most of the money being spent on stipends for teachers and for office staff. So directors spend much of their time during the year scurrying about for money. Typically, we have been funded through joint arrangements with the university and private foundations. We have had major support from the Martha Holden Jennings Foundation, the Scioto County Area Foundation, the National Endowment for the Humanities, and the Thomas J. Emery Foundation; we have received minor support from the Laub Foundation and the Hartzell-Norris Charitable Trust. Foundations have provided money for stipends and for staffing and office expenses, while the university has provided services and released time for the directors. In 1982, the National Diffusion Network, through the Ohio State Department of Education, funded the teacher stipends.

The Ohio Board of Regents' Early English Composition Assessment Program

Recently, the Ohio Writing Project became part of an articulation program, developed by the Ohio Board of Regents, called the Early English Composition Assessment Program. This new affiliation has considerably increased the size and scope of our enterprise. The combined Writing Project–EECAP program is funded through matching grants provided by the board of regents, the university, and local school districts. The regents and the university each contribute $30,000. The districts together must contribute at least $30,000 more. Before joining EECAP, our annual budget was $30,000–$40,000 per year. This year, it will reach almost $140,000. Before joining EECAP, we averaged thirty teachers per summer institute. In the summer of 1985, a total of eighty teachers from twenty-four districts attended three concurrent institute classes. The twenty-eight districts that have joined the 1985–86 program will send more than ninety teachers to the summer institute.

EECAP has also greatly changed the project's relationships—especially to the districts but to the university, to the state bureaucracy, and to individual teachers as well. In essence, the regents' program is designed to aid in the articulation of students from the state's high schools into universities. It provides funds to support the collaborative efforts of public schools and universities to evaluate and improve the writing skills of college-bound students and, ultimately, to improve the teaching of writing in the public schools. The core of EECAP is a program that tests and evaluates the writing of all junior-level students in participating districts.

Thus, the Ohio Writing Project is no longer simply a teacher-retraining program that offers a summer institute to which individual teachers apply and that contracts with individual districts for in-service programs but a joint teacher-retraining–articulation program that provides training, testing, and evaluation for teachers and students directly through collaborative school district–writing project contracts. Specifically, school districts join the program by sending at least three teachers to the summer institute and supporting them with stipends to cover tuition and expenses. In return, the Ohio Writing Project provides participating districts with teacher training, student testing and evaluation, and in-service and consulting. The separate parts of the joint program reinforce and enhance one another, each adding substance and motivation to the whole.

The Ohio Writing Project trains teachers through the summer institute to redesign school curricula, to teach grammar and writing classes, to design and satisfy pupil-performance objectives, and to assess student writing holistically and analytically. It provides participating districts with testing and evaluation for all their juniors. This testing and evaluation, of course, demanded a major addition to our teacher-training components and a major change in our relationship with teachers and school districts. Never before had we dealt with students directly. In 1984, forty-seven hundred juniors in the involved districts wrote hour-long essays that we graded both holistically and analytically in two weekend-long ETS-like sessions involving thirty-five teachers each. In 1985–86, we will grade over twelve thousand papers from juniors and seniors in participating districts.

After the grades are entered into the computer, students are sent individual evaluations, and schools and districts are sent summary profiles. The student evaluations assess individual strengths and weaknesses, with suggestions about how students might improve their own writing during their senior year in high school. The school and district evaluations synthesize the individual evaluations, suggesting composition areas district schools should focus on to improve their writing instruction.

The writing evaluations help to guide the consultation sessions between the project directors and the district teachers and administrators. Using those results, we plan the series of four in-service workshops that the project provides for each district. To take an obvious case, if district students score low in the analytic areas of coherence and supporting details, we suggest that the district plan an in-service workshop on coherence and another on the use of illustrations. If another school district finds its students score lowest on usage, we arrange to have all presentations concentrate on revising, editing, and correcting. (In actuality, of course, few consultations are as simple as our examples suggest. Since our negotiations and plans always rely on districts' special requests, politics and public relations often play a role in our in-service planning.) The consultation also includes providing districts with curriculum packets developed by teachers in the institute. These materials include objectives for performance in composition skills as well as writing assignments and suggestions about how to teach the skills outlined by the objectives.

Obviously, we attempt to be comprehensive. We think we succeed in meeting the goals of the separate components of the program. But we have our difficulties. Besides the administrative problems caused by the sudden growth of the project through EECAP (and before that the hassle of fund raising), our major substantive problem is one we share with most other writing projects: how best to balance practice and theory within the institute curriculum. Much of the National Writing Project philosophy centers on the contributions of the teachers— their sharing successful experiences, their sharing writing and editing, their sharing social activities. For instance, Sam Watson, the director of the North Carolina Writing Project, recently wrote that there are three essential activities for the summer institutes: "presentation of an effective teaching strategy by each member of the institute; regular meetings of small groups, where Fellows read and respond to each other's writing; and some sort of social occasion, held off campus each week."

No doubt such collegial activities are important for teachers and for the success of the institute. For one thing, they get teachers out of the classroom and talking with one another about the problems of teaching writing, and— often for the first time in their careers—sharing solutions to those problems. For another, they provide psychological support for individuals within the group. No one who has witnessed a reunion of teachers from a summer institute— with its hugging, backslapping, and general emotional outpouring—could question the important therapeutic effect of the collegiality. Shared problems, shared solutions, and shared emotions clearly make teachers happier with themselves as teachers and writers, and improved self-concepts most certainly lead to better teaching. Nonetheless, such experiences do not offer the coherent body of knowledge that can provide the intellectual stimulation for a course, the foundation for a discipline, or the framework for a profession. In essence, without an informing context for the institute, project teachers could return to their classrooms less frustrated but no more knowledgeable about teaching writing.

In an *Arizona English Bulletin* article several years ago, we argued that only through knowledge of a common core of works in language, cognition, and pedagogy can writing teachers become professionals. And we went on to argue that project sites should immerse elementary and secondary teachers in the emerging paradigm Hairston delimits, a shared body of knowledge and set of assumptions about writing and the teaching of writing. In our own summer institute, we give teachers large doses of reading in the literature of the profession—Peter Elbow, Donald Murray, Donald Graves, William Irmscher, Janet Emig, Kenneth Macrorie, Mina Shaughnessy, and others. We encourage the teachers to comment on the articles and books in their response journals, in whatever way they see fit. They may write letters to the authors, create dialogues among researchers, or wax lyrical in poetry. These journal entries become the starting points for class discussions. An anonymously scrawled poem on the blackboard about Peter Elbow "writing away . . . / . . . while cooking up words," for example, engenders an argument about the relative merits of free-writing and outlining. Later, a fictional argument between James Moffett and Richard Larson stimulates a debate on the effectiveness of teaching fluency or rhetorical forms. After such interplay among the teachers and between the teachers and the material, the teachers discover that their improved theoretical background can enhance their own presentations as well as their critical skills.

In several ways, the EECAP program has given new import to our emphasis on background theory and research. The grading sessions themselves, which take place in January, five months before the institute, bring to the fore questions about process and product, about the reality or importance of the modes of development (whether, for instance, narrative or expository papers best satisfy the assigned topic), and about the relation of correctness to the quality of the paper (this is the issue that demands the most careful handling by the leader of the evaluation session). Teachers who have argued these points while being trained as graders come into the institute more prepared to search for answers not only from one another but also within the professional literature. The grading sessions, therefore, produce subtle changes in the way the teachers think about writing even before they arrive on campus in June.

Not only does EECAP give new import to our emphasis on background theory and research, but our new relation to school districts through EECAP demands that the Ohio Writing Project disseminate to the districts models for state-mandated competency objectives on the writing skills of students from kindergarten through twelfth grade. So, in the 1984 summer institute, we had teachers work in groups, according to their grade levels, to arrive at objectives for the several grades that we could publish and distribute to participating districts. We encouraged teachers to come up with process- rather than product-oriented objectives, objectives based on their readings in language development, error analysis, and discourse theory, as well as their cumulative experience in the classroom.

Since 1980, the Ohio Writing Project has functioned as a site of the National Writing Project, and we still hold firmly to the notions that guide the worldwide network. We could never, of course, dismiss from our program its core identity with the National Writing Project. Our teachers will continue to teach one another because, as the National Writing Project claims, the best teacher of teachers *is* another teacher. They will continue to write and share their writing with one another. And—most crucial—they will continue to draw sustenance and renewed zest for teaching from a community of teachers who, like them, give up their summer to find better ways to teach students. Our identity, however, has evolved beyond that of a National Writing Project site. One different wrinkle in our program springs from our belief that the only access to true professionalism in any discipline is through rigorous intellectual inquiry. Accordingly, our teachers read widely and write about the rapidly growing body of professional literature on composition. Our emphasis on such hard-won professionalism merges nicely with our new alliance with the Ohio Board of Regents' Early English Composition Assessment Program. Ultimately, it is teachers at all levels, kindergarten through college, trained in every aspect of the discipline—in theory as well as pedagogy—who ensure true articulation within any state system of education.

Editor's note

The project described here illustrates how faculty at a National Writing Project site have accommodated the distinguishing features of the Bay Area Writing Project to their individual needs and have blended those features with their own school-college collaborative program.

Youngstown State University: The English Festival and Project ARETE

Barbara Brothers, Carol Gay, Gratia Murphy, and Gary Salvner

Concerned about the reading and writing abilities of our students at Youngstown State University and their knowledge and appreciation of literature and literary history, the English department began in 1974 to work with area teachers, kindergarten through twelfth grade. Our objectives were (and continue to be) to emphasize the importance of literature and of reading and writing and to work toward ways in which instruction and the curriculum might produce more literate students than those who were entering the university. The programs we sponsored that focus on literature for area teachers have effected changes not only in their teaching and curriculum but in our own as well. On the other hand, efforts to improve our own composition program have developed into specific programs for area schools in the teaching and assessment of writing. The informal assessment that we made of our students in 1974 demonstrated to us the need to offer remedial instruction in writing and to develop a test that would identify the students requiring that instruction. Becoming knowledgeable about research in the teaching of writing and about methods of assessing the writing skills of students enabled us to develop a more effective writing curriculum at the university and to aid the schools in improving their curricula. In collaboration with the schools, for example, we have undertaken "assessment and revitalization efforts for the teaching of English"—Project ARETE, described later in this report. Though cultivating collegiality between secondary and postsecondary teachers was not an initial objective, the spirit of mutual support, cooperation, and humility (we did not have all the answers) with which we entered into our endeavors has made that collegiality an outcome and a key ingredient in what successes we have had. We are learning from each other. English education is a profession of which we are all a part.

Background

The development and growth of our cooperative programs with the schools have been shaped, of course, by the structure and nature of our institution and department. Youngstown State University is a commuter school, an urban university that draws nearly ninety percent of its undergraduates from a tricounty area. Since we offer both the master of arts degree in English and a master teacher degree in English, we serve the educational needs of teachers as well. Two English faculty members hold cross appointments in the School of Education, and the department not only advises and supervises undergraduate student teachers but also offers courses in English education that are cross-listed as School of Education offerings.

Initially we chose to work with the schools by sponsoring in-service workshops for area teachers on the professional day sponsored each fall by the Northeastern Ohio Teachers Association (NEOTA). In 1974, we held a workshop on children's literature, organized by Carol Gay, an American literature specialist who taught children's literature; the sessions were led by university faculty members whose specializations ranged from Renaissance drama to the modern British novel. In 1975, we again sponsored a literature workshop, but through funds NEOTA had for the program, we secured as principal speaker Michael Slater, a Dickens scholar at Birkbeck College, University of London, and a Distinguished Visiting Professor at Ohio State University. Thus, besides having something of value to say to the grade school or high school teacher about our literary fields, this workshop enriched us and our teaching.

In addition, we involved some of the area teachers in planning and leading the workshops and discussion groups that were a part of that program. Our subsequent NEOTA programs, therefore, enabled school and university teachers not only to hear such scholars as Elisabeth McPherson, David Bleich, and Richard Beach and to consider what implications their ideas had for teaching writing and literature but also to get to know one another and to form professional ties. Our faculty became identified as an important resource, and various members were asked to conduct in-service workshops at the area schools, to serve on textbook selection and curriculum revision committees within the schools, and to speak to high school English classes about the literary works assigned in the course. Our NEOTA programs also gave us the model of cooperative planning and participation and of mutual learning that informs Project ARETE and the English Festival, also described below. And we invite the area teachers to university-funded presentations by scholars.

The NEOTA workshops also led to professional growth in our own classrooms. In our graduate classes we began to ask for papers with pedagogical as well as scholarly themes—a slide lecture on Yeats for high school students or a unit plan for teaching Chaucer or Shakespeare—and to give more and varied writing assignments for audiences other than scholars. We were asking ourselves what kinds of assignments would best contribute to the professional development of our students. We looked at our own curriculum to determine if it was meeting the needs of all our students: those who were practicing high school English teachers or who would become lower-division college instructors, those pursuing the MA as a foundation for even more advanced graduate work, those planning to use their acquired skills in other than academic occupations, and those seeking only personal enrichment. We revised the graduate curriculum to ensure that students would broaden as well as deepen their knowledge of literature, still the core of our program, and we expanded the course offerings in English education to include children's and adolescent literature and additional classes on the teaching of writing.

In 1976 we used our graduate class in the teaching of English to bring in selected schoolteachers of all grade levels for a summer workshop on the teaching of writing. The course was planned by H. Thomas McCracken, who regularly taught courses in English education, and Gratia Murphy, the director of composition, along with Barbara Brothers. We asked a number of other faculty members to make presentations, but we stipulated that they had to participate in the workshop, since we were all learning from one another. The following summer, using the same format, we held an advanced workshop on evaluating writing. A bibliography of sources on teaching and evaluating writing was compiled for the teachers who took the course, and that bibliography became a resource for our own composition teachers. Having seen the value of coming together to consider research, problems, and strategies related to teaching writing, we also initiated a fall workshop for our own teachers, including limited-service and full-service faculty members and graduate assistants. In addition, we required our graduate assistants to take the teaching-of-writing course and to participate in a year-long noncredit practicum to prepare them for their initial teaching assignments. The introduction to composition and theory course and a seminar on problems and issues in teaching writing instruct teachers at all levels.

Since a large number of area high school students enroll at YSU, we made the students' English placement test results available to their high school counselors. In addition to the Nelson-Denny Reading Test, the English placement test consists of two writing tasks, a sentence-combining and editing exercise and a brief original composition on a focused topic. The schools thus became aware that we assessed the writing abilities of their college-bound students and that we based the assessment on the students' writing rather than on answers to multiple-choice questions. We had clearly signaled the need for better writing instruction and demonstrated the inadequacy of using grammar drills and tests to teach and evaluate writing.

The Writing Center, which we established to help meet the students' needs for remedial and supplemental instruction and for tutorial help in writing for their other courses, served as a model for area schools, some of which established their own writing centers and others of which called on us to identify resources useful for remedial instruction in writing.

To further our knowledge of the problems the English teachers in the schools were facing, the director of freshman composition spent her sabbatical teaching half days in each of the five city high schools. During the year she applied for a basic-skills grant from the Ohio Department of Education to fund presentations by university faculty members in a series of afternoon workshops for the Youngstown English teachers.

Other programs we directed that have been funded, at least in part, by grants from the Ohio State Department of Education include institutes for the Youngstown public and parochial school systems and a Trumbull County institute to prepare teachers to integrate the teaching of writing, reading, speaking, and listening into a new high school curriculum to replace the old elective mini-courses. Colleges and universities that wish to work with the schools should keep abreast of the grants available to the public schools and to departments or schools of education and should be aware that those grants change, often from year to year. They also should know about the funds within the local school districts for teacher development and should see that some of those funds go toward giving English teachers the time and help they need for curriculum and instruction development.

Institutions, like YSU, that attract students from a limited geographical area gain, of course, by having better prepared freshmen, freshmen who are more likely to stay in school and to graduate. Our community (the schools, the university, and the public) has a heightened sense of the importance of writing and literature, and our cooperative efforts have improved our instruction and curriculum. By joining hands, not pointing fingers of blame, we are enhancing the literacy not only of the students who enter our university but also of those who leave it.

The Youngstown State University English Festival

The YSU English Festival was conceived in the fall of 1978 when two members of the English department decided to establish a memorial fund to reward students in junior and senior high schools for distinctive writing based on careful reading. The program that grew out of this initial desire was prompted by the department's long-standing interest in furthering fruitful communication between area schools and the university. The department endorsed the awards and appointed a committee of five faculty members to establish a format. Before long, an advisory board of area educators and community leaders had been set up to aid in planning and in defining objectives, and an entire program of reading and writing activities had been devised.

Since that first festival in the spring of 1979, the program has steadily grown from 550 students and teachers coming to the campus for a day's activities based on reading and writing to a three-day program drawing over 2,400 students and 400 teachers and parents from over ninety-nine schools in a five-county area. The advisory board has grown to twenty members, and this year over 150 area teachers actively participated in the festival, either as presenters or as judges. In addition, seven YSU faculty members served on the festival committee and another twenty-five took an active part in the program.

The English Festival is unique because its student participants—average students as well as honor students—must read the seven carefully chosen books on the annual festival booklist in order to be excused from their classes at school to spend a full day on the YSU campus engaging in various competitions and activities centering on the booklist. Students who begin attending the festival in the seventh grade and who attend each year thereafter will have read forty-two festival books by the time they graduate.

Each day the thousands of essays and other forms of writing done at the festival are evaluated by teachers trained in both holistic and primary-trait reading. At the daily awards ceremony, well over three hundred winners are given certificates and various prizes contributed by publishing houses and numerous area business firms and community groups.

Objectives

All teachers and students wishing to attend the English Festival receive a brochure stating the project's objectives: (1) to provide an exciting and stimulating setting for enjoyable and worthwhile reading and writing activities, (2) to support teachers who emphasize reading and writing in the classroom, (3) to offer models for effective classroom activities, (4) to involve the whole community in fostering good reading and writing skills, (5) to recognize and reward distinctive writing, and (6) to introduce students to a wide variety of superior books covering a broad range of interests.

Program Structure

The English Festival works in the following way. All students attend a talk by a nationally recognized author (e.g., Joan Blos, 1983; William Sleator, 1984; M. E. Kerr, 1985) and take a book quiz that helps determine whether or not they have read the seven books required for participation in the festival and tests their skill at remembering details. They can also take part in a variety of other activities: impromptu writing contests and writing games, which not only cultivate reading and writing skills but also encourage students to think creatively, follow directions, and draw effective generalizations; language games, which enable them to work with important principles of language in a game situation; prose, poetry, and journalism workshops; writing labs, which give them experience in group writing; and insight sessions, where they get a chance to discuss specific books with their peers as well as with a group leader, who can be a university faculty member, an area teacher with exceptional classroom skills, or a faculty member from another university. In addition, they can witness dramatic or media presentations. The day culminates with the awarding of prizes for achievements in the various competitions. The excitement of a festival awards ceremony rivals that of a basketball game, with schools cheering students who have demonstrated reading and writing skill rather than athletic ability—a pleasant change of focus.

Teachers can attend a discussion and question-and-answer session with the guest author; hear a specialist talk about a problem of interest to teachers, parents, and librarians (e.g., James Davis of Ohio University on the topic "Open Book: Open Mind"); participate in judging sessions in holistic and primary-trait scoring; learn new teaching strategies by attending any of the sessions scheduled for students; and hear the guest author address the students.

Teachers and students have responded to the festival with such eagerness that, though we bring 2,400 students to campus each year, we turn away more than we can accept. Because we have always approached area teachers as colleagues, cooperation with area schools has been extraordinarily positive. While teachers are sometimes hesitant to lead discussions, they welcome serving as writing-lab coleaders, along with university faculty members, and as judges, an experience they find valuable and enjoyable. Further, teachers and administrators are eager to serve on the advisory board, which takes an active part in determining policy and solving administrative problems.

Current Problems

The main problem the department has faced with the festival program is its overwhelming success. The large number of schools wanting to participate puts a great strain on the faculty and on university facilities. True, we have had help: grants from B. Dalton Bookseller, the Ohio Humanities Council, and Bank One of Ohio bring guest speakers and resource people from other universities, area businesses have generously donated prizes (over $5,000 in 1984), and the university absorbs the printing and secretarial costs. Still, those who administer the program or participate in it receive no released time. Since almost three-fourths of the English department's full-time staff take part in the activities and since seven members serve on the festival committee, working an average of three hours per week, the commitment of the department has reached its limits. Since our festival cannot grow bigger, the committee has prepared a slide show and information packets to encourage area schools to sponsor their own "minifestivals" and to demonstrate to other interested universities and high schools how to create and administer their own programs. Two colleges, Otterbein in Ohio and Delta in Michigan, have established festivals modeled after YSU's with much the same success and enthusiastic response.

Plans

As for the future, since the general outline of the program—both in its goals and in its organization—has been successful, we do not anticipate any great changes. We are moving toward greater parent participation by actively involving parents as well as students in group discussions of the books, inviting parents to serve as monitors and judges and encouraging them to get used to the idea of sharing literature with their children. We intend to bring in more resource people from other universities and high schools outside the area to provide classroom models of teaching activities and to keep area teachers abreast of current theory and practice in teaching reading and writing. Books of professional interest are awarded to the schools of the top essay winners. Finally, to recognize outstanding critical writing by teachers and to identify and reward the skills and knowledge that make for outstanding teaching in the secondary schools, the chairperson of the English department offers an annual prize, begun in 1985, for the best critical essay about a festival book written by a teacher from a participating school.

Our main concern for the future is maintaining the high level of success, the efficient organization, and the exciting sense of enthusiasm that the festival has achieved in the past.

Project ARETE

Our assessment and revitalization efforts for the teaching of English—Project ARETE—would never have been implemented, perhaps not even conceived, if the avenues of communication between the English department and the area secondary schools had not already been in place. In September 1983, the Ohio Board of Regents (OBOR) announced the availability of funds for the Early English Composition Assessment Program (EECAP) to help Ohio's public high schools and state-supported universities work together to reduce the need for remedial writing instruction at the university. In the academic year 1982–83, our department had already tested juniors in the five public and two parochial high schools for composition skills and helped the Youngstown school system develop a curriculum guide for English IV, a course designed for college-bound seniors who had scored badly in their junior year. Therefore, when OBOR offered up to $30,000 a year for a two-year period, money to be matched by the school districts and the university, we agreed to work with the schools in Youngstown again and to add the fourteen Mahoning County high schools. Project ARETE was funded, with Gratia Murphy and Gary Salvner as project directors the first year and Gratia Murphy and John Mason the second. The project involved thirty-six high school teachers, two curriculum specialists in the Youngstown and Mahoning school systems, five faculty consultants from the English department, and a consultant from the state department of education. The chairperson of the English department and the directors of instruction from Mahoning County and the Youngstown public schools participated in both planning and implementing the project.

Objectives

Project ARETE has two specific objectives: first, to help schools learn how to assess the writing of their students reliably and efficiently; and second, building on that assessment, to shape curricular changes and classroom methods to produce more effective composition instruction in the local secondary schools. The project seeks to cultivate collegiality and communication between university and high school instructors. For example, teachers were trained to administer a large-scale writing test in their schools and, after an intensive introduction to two techniques of assessment (holistic and trait) and some practice sessions, scored the 3,088 writing samples of the juniors in the nineteen high schools. The teachers worked with the project directors and the faculty consultants to develop and refine their own trait scoring guide, identifying and describing the five qualities of writing they deemed important (purpose, direction, ideas, style, and presentation) and the characteristics of high, middle, and low performances in each of these qualities. Both high school and university teachers have profited from this collegial discussion of writing. High school teachers welcomed the additional access to research and theory that university teachers have, and university faculty members became aware of some of the practical teaching-load, schedule, and curriculum problems that high school teachers face.

Structure and Procedures

The activities of Project ARETE are related to its two objectives of large-scale assessment of student writing and revitalized composition instruction in the secondary schools. To provide the sample for assessment, all juniors in the nineteen high schools wrote a two-part examination similar to our English placement test: a sentence-combining and editing task and an original essay. Teachers read all samples (coded by student and school numbers) holistically, rating them on a scale of 1 to 4. Results were returned to the schools, showing student performance in both parts of the test, so that guidance counselors could direct students into proper courses for their senior year, particularly those students who had indicated they were college-bound. Students also completed a six-question attitudinal survey on writing and reading. Following the holistic scoring, forty percent of the 3,088 original essays were assessed on the five qualities teachers had outlined. Fourteen schools chose to use random selection, while the five Youngstown schools asked to use their college-bound students as the sample for this second, analytic scoring. After workshops devoted to the writing of the scoring guide, the teachers read the essays, marking them on a continuum of 1 to

7 for each of the five qualities outlined, with 1–2 scores being "low," 3–5 "middle," and 6–7 "high." Each essay received two readings, and a third reading if the first scores differed by four or more points. Essays were collated with their scoring slips, scores were tabulated, and reports showing means and performances in each of the five qualities for both the school and the system were returned to the school administrators. During the second year of the project, juniors were again tested (being asked only to write an original essay), and all papers were evaluated according to the trait scoring guide.

To meet the second objective, improved instruction, twenty-five participants, five university faculty consultants, and the project directors convened in a forty-hour workshop in June 1984 to write a draft of a composition resource manual. This manual explains in detail the five qualities used in trait scoring, offers annotated papers that show varying degrees of competence with regard to those qualities, includes theoretical discussions and relevant research, and provides sample teaching strategies for each quality. The manual was revised, edited, and class-tested during 1984–85 and made available to all high school English teachers in the nineteen schools for use as a resource guide for teaching. Because teachers themselves developed this resource, titled *Teacher to Teacher*, it has been accepted enthusiastically.

Problems

At this point in Project ARETE, our offices show the enormous amount of paper storing, organizing, shuffling, and recording that a project of this size requires, and we have had to add clerical help (although little could be done about space). More substantially, we have discovered places where we can make our procedures more efficient and our scoring guide easier for teachers to use. A computer program now does the time-consuming collating of readers' scores and prepares individualized letters giving results to students and statistical reports for teachers, schools, and districts. The biggest problem—and one that even technology cannot solve—is that both university and high school teachers lack the time to do all we had hoped. Although each project director has a teaching-load reduction of four hours per quarter, teachers are not free to meet until after the school day, and because of their busy schedules of teaching and supervising extracurricular activities, the project has meant long hours for all participants.

Plans

Project ARETE's immediate future is fairly well set, since our second proposal outlined in detail activities through 1987, OBOR having offered an additional two years of funding for ARETE. In addition to assessing the writing of all juniors in Youngstown and Mahoning County schools, we are assessing some ninth-grade students' writing. Test administrators are being trained within the schools so that the schools themselves can continue assessment after Project ARETE ends in 1987.

The revitalization efforts of the project also continue. *Teacher to Teacher* will be expanded and revised once more during the last year of the project. Project directors and university consultants from the English department are working with schools to revise courses of study and curricula in written composition. Model units, prepared by teams of high school teachers and a YSU faculty consultant, are being distributed to all secondary English teachers at in-service workshops, and at least one retreat is planned to coordinate assessment and teaching efforts. A regional convention on assessing and teaching writing is planned for the spring of 1987 as a culminating activity for Project ARETE. Presentations will be made by both area teachers and university faculty members.

The Ohio State Department of Education has mandated that by the fall of 1987 schools must have a system of assessing writing competence at least three times during a student's twelve years of instruction. Although Project ARETE was not designed to meet this obligation, the methods of assessment we have developed are usable and reliable, and numbers of teachers have been trained in them.

We have had some inquiries about expanding our base to include other area schools; although we have not yet made a decision, the geographical spread of teachers and schools makes group meetings and reading sessions inconvenient, if not impossible.

Recommendation

One of the most surprising outcomes of Project ARETE has been the evidence of the continuing need for clear communication between secondary schools and universities. No matter how many cooperative projects or activities are undertaken, the need to go on talking and working together remains strong. It is amazing how much misinformation about the university and its expectations and procedures is current. High school teachers "know" about college programs and practices through their returning students, who often present an inaccurate or incomplete portrayal. That teachers are working together, sharing information, and clarifying the competencies and the experience that universities expect from incoming students is the most positive outcome of Project ARETE. It is also a signal that avenues of communication must be kept open, even—or especially—when projects such as ours are over. The fostering of collegiality and cooperation is important enough to teachers and students alike to make it a university activity of highest priority.

University of Southern California: The Huntington Beach Project Literacy

W. Ross Winterowd

In October 1976, the Huntington Beach Union High School District in California commissioned me to establish a literacy project in six high schools. Working with my colleague and student, Dorothy Augustine of Chapman College, I proposed an intricate plan to the district, and Superintendent Frank Abbott, Assistant Superintendent John Gyves, and the board gave us the go-ahead. Much of this essay is based on our experiences with and evaluations of the Huntington Beach project. The effectiveness of this plan is suggested by a report of the Huntington Beach Union High School District on its ninth-grade writing program. The report is too long to reproduce here, but I want to call attention to four paragraphs from its "Summary and Conclusions":

> The data presented in this report show that, on the average, posttest writing scores were substantially higher than pretest writing scores. The gains were much higher among students showing low pretest performance. This may, in part, be accounted for by normal regression effects. However, the 1977–78 gains for this group are considerably higher than those for the 1976–77 comparable group suggesting greater program impact. The same conclusion holds for the total ninth grade population.
>
> The performance of the students at W[estminster] H[igh] S[chool] is most encouraging. This performance is contradictory to what is generally seen in test results in the district (WHS is normally the lowest scoring school), but repeats the 1976–77 finding of WHS scoring at the top. The two years of consistent data would certainly suggest a program strength at WHS.
>
> The dramatic turnaround of student performance at O[cean] V[iew] H[igh] S[chool] is also very encouraging, particularly for the total ninth grade. This change would suggest that OVHS found or developed instructional techniques that are highly effective.
>
> The strength of performance at WHS and OVHS would indicate that the remaining schools could benefit by reviewing their programs in terms of those at WHS and OVHS.

The Huntington Beach model has been adapted for and adopted at the University of Southern California. It is a model that has been successful and that is now ready to be adopted, *mutatis mutandis*, by other secondary schools or by colleges and universities around the country.

Objectives

The objectives of the program can be expressed as a series of values that the program attempts to instill in the teachers who participate in it. The values I am speaking of are an integral part of our efforts on the secondary and college levels: authority, commitment, and what I choose to call beneficence.

A faculty needs a sense of authority, not conferred by a dean, superintendent, or a board, but arising from the members' sense that they know their field, that they understand what they are doing, that they are genuine professionals. It is paradoxical that the academy—universities that train teachers of reading and writing—typically bestow authority in the wrong field. By and large, the secondary and college teachers of reading and writing have gained authority in the study of literature, in interpretation, the history of ideas, biography, and so on. The authority that teachers have is a paradox precisely because teachers of reading and writing are not so much concerned with a text as with the processes whereby a text is constructed by a writer and subsequently reconstructed by a reader. It might be said that the knowledge of literature is mainly a knowledge of texts and that the knowledge of literacy is mainly a knowledge of processes. I am not claiming that these two bodies of knowledge are mutually exclusive, but they are quite obviously not identical. To have authority, a teacher of writing, then, must know about language acquisition, a requirement that takes one at least to linguistics, psychology, and anthropology. A teacher without authority is always a victim. A teacher with spurious authority victimizes. Obviously one effort of any literacy program must be to confer genuine authority on teachers.

I will say less about commitment and beneficence, though I believe that they are crucial values for a teacher. Commitment is disinterested allegiance to a field. Beneficence is humane concern for the relationship between the field and the students. The authority without commitment is likely to be an authoritarian cynic whose self-confidence in the field of endeavor translates into browbeating and clever showmanship. The teacher with commitment and beneficence but without authority is quite likely to be extremely effective with most students, with the easy cases, but will be ineffective with the students who need to be taught (who, unlike the easy cases, do not simply learn) and disastrously inept at planning or supervision, activities that often involve the spending of large sums of money for textbooks, equipment, in-service training, and so on.

Structure

The Huntington Beach literacy program can be subdivided into two broad but intricately interrelated phases: training and application. The preservice and inservice training in the high school district and at the university have as their rationale the conferring of authority on teachers. This authority, of course, comes from knowledge, and the knowledge itself results in know-how or methodology. Knowledge is strategic, providing a coherent framework for a set of extremely complex activities that extend over a semester, a year, four years, and that vary from student to student. Know-how is tactical; it is the application of knowledge in a scene, to solve a given problem with a certain student at some time. Knowledge confers authority. Without knowledge, know-how is an incoherent set of gimmicks that may or may not work most of the time but that can never serve as the basis for a program.

It will perhaps be useful to outline the in-service training program that Dorothy Augustine and I developed for the Huntington Beach Union High School District and that in substance is very much like the preservice and in-service training program at USC.

The in-service training program initially focuses on the questions "What sorts of knowledge do teachers of literacy, and particularly of writing, need?" and "How do they best gain that knowledge?" The preparation begins with the most basic considerations of written composition as a rhetorical act, as a writer with a semantic intention to convey to an audience that is always more or less hypothetical in some more or less specific scene. According to my definition, any discourse act, written or spoken, is the projection of a semantic intention through structures to an audience in a scene. Writing teachers need to know and think about ethical (writer-centered), pathetic (audience-centered), and logical arguments; about style; about form or arrangement; and particularly about the ratios among these factors in the discourse act.

It happens that ordinary language philosophy (with its explorations of illocutionary and perlocutionary force), literary theory (with its recent emphasis on literature in the reader rather than on the page), psychology, linguistics, and other fields (not to mention real rhetoric, such as that of Burke, Booth, and others, as opposed to the pseudorhetoric of the composition handbook) all bear on and clarify this elegant set of concerns with audience, stance, style, form, and deduction and induction that pretty much define what the field of rhetoric has been in the past and is to a large extent at present. To put trainees in touch with the field of rhetoric and the questions that it asks, we used my own *Contemporary Rhetoric: A Conceptual Background with Readings* (New York: Harcourt, 1975).

Once this framework of rhetoric has been established, other components of the preparation fit nicely. As I said earlier, writing teachers need—and invariably find useful—something more than a lay person's knowledge of language: sociolinguistics, psycholinguistics (particularly language-acquisition and split-brain theory), and some syntax and grammatical theory. In Huntington Beach, for instance, teachers worked their way through Nancy Ainsworth Johnson's *Current Topics in Language: Introductory Readings* (Cambridge: Winthrop, 1976); William Labov's now classic *The Study of Nonstandard English* (Urbana: NCTE, 1970); Frank O'Hare's *Sentence Combining: Improving Student Writing without Formal Grammar Instruction* (Urbana: NCTE, 1973); and some other pieces (such as an unpublished paper on cerebral hemisphericity and Walter Loban's *Language Development, K–12* [Urbana: NCTE, 1976]). As I will explain, Stephen Krashen's monitor theory of second language learning is important in our work, and trainees read two of his manuscript papers on the theory, now published as "Second Language Acquisition," *Personal Viewpoints on Aspects of ESL*, ed. M. Burt et al. (New York: Regents, 1976) and "On the Acquisition of Planned Discourse: Written English as a Second Dialect," in *Proceedings of the Claremont Reading Conference* (Claremont, 1978).

Of course, front-line teachers do not have unlimited time, and assuredly they are in one of the most energy-draining of all professions; therefore, in Huntington Beach my colleague and I did not hesitate to summarize important works to provide a broad background, a context, for the specific readings that the trainees did. Furthermore, we attempted to convey that the work we were doing was at the cutting edge of knowledge in the field. We discussed the Loban monograph shortly after it was published; we discussed the monitor theory and hemisphericity papers before they were published. And all of us, I think, gained the sense that we are in a developing field and that, as a consequence, any knowledge we acquire will be forever just a beginning. No longer, then, can anyone who needs authority in the field stop being a learner (i.e., a scholar) on earning a degree and entering the profession.

The in-service training program stresses the importance of helping teachers translate the knowledge they develop into the know-how they need in the classroom. All the know-how in our composition programs at Huntington Beach and the University of Southern California relates to one of the following categories: (1) prewriting, (2) composing, (3) reformulating, and (4) editing. Prewriting includes all the activities that go into formulating a preliminary semantic intention (in terms of classical rhetoric, "invention"); composing is the expression of that intention in structures (sentences, paragraphs, etc.); reformulating involves changing structures to express the semantic intention more cogently or to change that intention; and editing is the process of adjusting the "surface" of the text so that it approximates, more or less nearly, the only national written "dialect," Edited Standard English. It is necessary, then, that teachers have effective techniques to intervene in and facilitate the subprocesses of the composing process. The writing teacher needs specific know-how.

In regard to prewriting, our know-how relies heavily on heuristics and the journal. Among other sources, we have drawn our techniques from James Adams, *Conceptual Blockbusting* (2nd ed., New York: Norton, 1979); D. Gordon Rohman and Albert O. Wlecke, *Prewriting: The Construction and Application of Models for Concept Formation in Writing* (East Lansing: Michigan State UP, 1964); Kenneth Burke, *A Grammar of Motives* (Berkeley: U of California P, 1969); Richard E. Young, Alton L. Becker, and Kenneth L. Pike, *Rhetoric: Discovery and Change* (New York: Harcourt, 1970); Edward de Bono, *Lateral Thinking: Creativity Step by Step* (New York: Harper, 1970); and Roman Jakobson, "Linguistics and Poetics," *Style in Language*, ed. Thomas A. Sebeok (Cambridge: MIT P, 1960). These heuristics (techniques of invention, problem definition, and problem solving) range from the simple to the complex, and they are adaptable to individual students or to given populations of students. So far, our widest experience is at the secondary level, but we do have evidence for the effectiveness of heuristics in college.

Know-how in teaching composing involves (among other concerns) syntactic fluency and, to a lesser extent, paragraph form. The knowledge concerning syntactic fluency comes from psycholinguistic studies that demonstrate the nature of language and its basis in the simple proposition and the combining of propositions into multilevel sentences and from studies of how gains in fluency affect student writing. The know-how is in sets of materials that teachers have available: for example, William Strong's *Sentence Combining* (New York: Random, 1973), Frank O'Hare's *Sentencecraft* (Lexington: Ginn, 1975), *The Christensen Method* (New York: Harper, 1968), and the syntactic-fluency program in W. Ross Winterowd and Patricia Y. Murray's *English Writing and Skills* (6 vols., San Diego: Coronado, 1985). Know-how on the paragraph is more nebulous and less varied and rich. For "basic writing" students, we use techniques drawn largely from concepts developed by Alton Becker in "A Tagmemic Approach to Paragraph Analysis," *The Sentence and the Paragraph* (Urbana: NCTE, 1965) and Francis Christensen, "A Generative Rhetoric of the Paragraph," *Notes toward a New Rhetoric* (New York: Harper, 1967). Beyond the sentence, know-how becomes less and less specific and merges with knowledge. For instance, in dealing with the coherence of whole essays, we have just begun to apply the principles of discourse analysis, but that field is still emerging and has not yet been shaken down into specific techniques and materials. Here is one place, in fact, where training in literary analysis can be especially valuable to teachers of writing, for people who have dealt with texts in detail have gained tacit knowledge of how these texts hang together, knowledge that can be translated into know-how on the spot.

Reformulating is clearly an important process, and to teach it effectively the instructor must have knowledge of how texts work in general. In our programs, that knowledge translates into some fairly simple know-how. Any act of reformulation must be one of the following: deletion, addition, rearrangement, or substitution of words, phrases, sentences, paragraphs, or sections. With that much background, plus a sensitivity to the complexities of texts, teachers can give students a powerful skill.

As for editing, writers must be able, when the occasion (i.e., audience or scene) demands, to approximate the surface structure of Edited Standard English. Know-how, then, is nothing more than the ability to give students the necessary skills—at the proper time and in the proper place. It is important to stress that the features of Edited Standard English (e.g., punctuation) are coherent systems and that it is therefore most effective to teach them as systems, not at random. In other words, if students cannot punctuate, they need to grasp the system of punctuation as a whole, not to correct random errors in this paper or that. It is also important to understand that the skills of editing are independent of audience and scene. They gain value for certain audiences in a given scene.

To facilitate the translation of the knowledge and know-how gained through the in-service program, we have created in the Huntington Beach high schools two scenes for instruction in writing: the writing workshop and the language-skills laboratory. Roughly characterized, the writing workshop is rhetorically charged with values and with the concerns of audience and scene; it is unsystematic, "messy," unpredictable. The laboratory is arhetorical, systematic, neat. In general, the workshop teaches prewriting, composing, and reformulating, whereas the laboratory teaches editing. This way of distributing instructional tasks and goals makes good sense, but in practice the cut is not quite so clean as one might assume.

The workshop-laboratory arrangement of instructional scenes results from the influence of various theories and bodies of knowledge. For example, we believe that discourse takes place and is learned most effectively in a rhetorical situation or scene, the necessary elements for which are at least exigency (a need, a situation that can be changed through discourse), audience, and constraints that approximate those of the real world (as opposed to the classroom world) as nearly as possible. We have tried to create in the workshops, then, a scene or situation in which learning to write would approximate as nearly as possible, and as frequently as possible, a real-world, out-of-school situation. The laboratory—with its programs and drills—obviously resembles nothing in the real world of language use, and that is one good reason for keeping it separate from the workshop.

In fact, a great deal of theory and a growing body of empirical evidence lie behind our decision to create these two learning scenes; monitor theory is particularly significant in this respect. Stephen Krashen, my colleague at USC who has developed monitor theory in his study of second language learning (and learning to compose seems to us, in many ways, like learning a second language), sees two kinds of learning occur as a student develops a command of a second language. The first sort of learning Krashen calls *acquisition*, and the second he terms *learning*.

> The technical term *acquisition* is here used to refer to the way linguistic abilities are internalized "naturally," that is, without conscious focusing on linguistic form. It appears to require, minimally, participation in natural communication situations, and is the way children gain knowledge of first and second languages. . . .
>
> Language acquisition is a subconscious process. Language *learning*, on the other hand, is a conscious process, and is the result of either a formal language learning situation or a self-study program. Formal learning situations are characterized by the process of feedback or error correction, absent in acquisition environments, and "rule isolation," the presentation of artificial linguistic environments that introduce just one new aspect of grammar at a time.

The result of learning is the construction of a *monitor* that allows the user consciously to regularize or correct output:

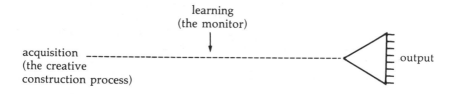

Now we can define the workshop as a place for acquiring compositional skills (prewriting, composing, reformulating) and the laboratory as a place for learning editing skills.

As for the physical scenes themselves—the places where workshop and editing skills are taught—the laboratory at least is not so much a place as a concept. It is a given kind of instruction for certain goals. In fact, two of the most effective laboratories in Huntington Beach look like this. Lab 1 is a file cabinet on wheels, which the teacher can move from room to room throughout the day. In this cabinet are exercises on photocopied sheets—some of them adapted from existing sources, some of them devised by the teacher herself, all of them fitting a general framework or inventory of monitor skills that was compiled when the Huntington Beach project first got under way. Lab 1 is literally wheeled into the space where the workshop is being held. Lab 2 is a separate room. (Here a good deal of individual conferencing goes on, often concerned with prewriting, composing, and reformulating, none of which is amenable to the systematic neatness of the monitor.) For observers who expect to find an electronic wonderland in a good laboratory, this place must be a terrible disappointment, for

its "equipment" is nothing but some two dozen cardboard boxes, filled with photocopied exercises and arranged according to an inventory of monitor skills. In
lab 1, the teacher is also the workshop teacher; in lab 2, the teacher does primarily
laboratory work, the students having been referred by workshop teachers in
the school.

The workshop and its interaction with the laboratory could best be described
with a videotape that would demonstrate, not tell about. However, a picture
of the workshop can be presented. Here is a montage of the kinds of things that
go on there:

1. Discussion of and practice with prewriting techniques by the whole class
2. Small-group activities—e.g., two students responding to and making suggestions regarding a paper (perhaps a rough draft) produced by a third student
3. Composing on the board, with volunteers making attempts to solve a given
   writing problem—e.g., getting a paper by one member of the class under way
   effectively
4. Whole-class discussion of one, two, or three photocopied papers produced by
   class members
5. Conferencing, the teacher circulating about the class to help individual students with writing problems while the other members of the class work on
   their papers
6. Some editing lessons for the whole class, dealing with a limited problem that
   all have in common
7. Reformulation exercises, in which all the class members make suggestions for
   improving one of their fellows' papers
8. Class discussion of audience, the adjustment of a given paper for a certain
   audience
9. Free-writing
10. Journal writing
11. Language games, such as the round-robin sentence, in which students succes-
    sively add modifiers to a base, perhaps (depending on the class's level of sophisti-
    cation) in the attempt to parody some author such as Faulkner
12. Publishing activities, in which groups of students or the whole class partici-
    pate in getting a collection ready for the "press" and distribution
13. Class development of writing assignments, during which students devise topics,
    define audiences, and delineate situations

The workshop is a messy place, highly charged, purposive in the sense of writing something for someone for some reason. When it becomes obvious that the
student's semantic intention must be given a surface structure to "reach" a certain audience in a scene, the laboratory assignment becomes meaningful. Because editing skills are put into a context, students grasp their importance.

If my pictures of the laboratory and the workshop have been at all clear,
then it should be apparent that knowledge translates itself into know-how in
these two learning scenes. The workshop is much nearer to an art studio in spirit
and operation than it is to a traditional English class. Within the framework
of goals and strategies, the students are working on their individual projects
under the guidance of a skilled teacher and with the cooperation of their
classmates.

Staffing

Fifteen or twenty teachers from the six high schools in the Huntington Beach Union District were involved in planning and establishing the program. Of these, a smaller group became a "hard-core" cadre: Christine Rice (Westminster High School), Julie Mayer (Westminster High School), John Nixon (Ocean View High School), Catherine McGough (Fountain Valley High School), Alida Moss (Edison High School), Joanne Haukland (Westminster High School), Richard Morley (Ocean View High School), Barbara Crane (Ocean View High School), and Susan Hales (Edison High School).

Beyond the twenty or so teachers who identified themselves as project people, attitudes ranged from hostility through indifference to enthusiasm and active support. Under administrative pressure to do *something*, a few teachers regressed more adamantly to the five-paragraph essay and "grammar"; others adopted or adapted "the Garrison method," "the Golden West College model," or "a systems approach to writing instruction." By and large, however, the Project Literacy model influenced the vast majority of English teachers in the district, and, after eight years, has become very much institutionalized, domesticated, naturalized; it is simply the way things work, not an intrusion, as many viewed the whole scheme when we proposed it in 1976.

Recommendations

In most secondary schools, English teachers are isolated from the contacts, activities, and rewards that energize a university faculty. It is a sad fact that teachers (especially English teachers) rank low on the scale of prestige. The problem of demoralization must be overcome if any educational program is to be successful. There must be rewards, and even though salary is important, professional rewards always transcend dollars and provide the stimulus that creates a good faculty.

The first necessity, then, is to give teachers professional stature, which comes about from engaging in professional activities that go beyond teaching. Publications, research, attending professional meetings, consulting within or outside the district—these are just some of the opportunities that raise teachers' images of themselves and that engage them totally in their profession. These opportunities are hard to create, however, if a faculty is isolated from the scholarly community at large, and therefore a university connection is essential. Simply, a school district should establish a close relationship with a college or university that shares professional interests with the schools' faculties. And I cannot stress this point enough. If such ties are established, the university has a readily accessible base for research, and the schools have the resources of university faculty members. The resulting collegiality brings teachers perforce into the professional circle.

The changes that I have talked about do not come easily or overnight. They cannot be brought about by administrative fiat. Furthermore, teachers are understandably cynical: a consultant comes into the district, gives a rousing Saturday workshop, and then disappears; the superintendent issues a mandate concerning accountability or declining test scores, and then, in effect, he too disappears; the state spends millions of dollars on new textbooks, and in class-rooms, north to south, the books disappear under the dust on shelves; a teacher has a breakthrough and the urge to share it with colleagues, but he or she seldom has the opportunity to appear. A nucleus of professionals does not disappear, and month by month teacher after teacher becomes more and more attracted to the project.

Finally, here is some practical advice about establishing a literacy project:

1. Find someone in authority who is sympathetic: an administrator, board member, someone on the city council. Talk to that person to gain access to the decision maker or makers.
2. Once access is gained, present a clear-cut and relatively simple proposal.
3. Make it clear that not much money is involved. There is nothing to buy except the time of the people involved.
4. When you get the mandate to proceed, carefully identify a relatively small group of faculty members who will work with you to get the project under way.
5. Make a realistic one-year plan, and in that plan make projections about the continuation of the project in the second year. (In the second year, project toward the third, and so on.) Insofar as the project is successful, it will eventually cease to be a project and will become a way of life, but until that happens it takes conscious effort and planning to keep the momentum up.

Further, the project can succeed only if the university and public school faculty members interact as peers rather than as guru and disciples. And there must be a "payoff" for teachers: the chance to publish in professional journals; consultancies in school districts and at colleges and universities; freedom from administrative control of programs, methods, and materials—in short, the kinds of perquisites, responsibilities, and opportunities that make university faculty positions attractive.

In Huntington Beach, we have been conducting this literacy project since 1976. We have also conducted in-service workshops on this project throughout the United States, and we have developed a comprehensive project manual that will serve as a guide to other districts and to colleges and universities that adopt or adapt the Huntington Beach model. Perhaps the single most happy result of the Huntington Beach project is that all of us enjoy it enormously—because we are seeing results and because we have become colleagues and friends.

Note

Reprinted, with revisions and adaptations, from *Reinventing the Rhetorical Tradition*, ed. Aviva Freedman and Ian Pringle (Conway, AR: L&S Books for the CCTE, 1980), copyright by the Canadian Council of Teachers of English and reprinted by permission.

National Endowment for the Humanities: Humanities Instruction in Elementary and Secondary Schools Program

Carolynn Reid-Wallace

This essay presents an overview of the Humanities Instruction in Elementary and Secondary Schools Program, a unit within the National Endowment for the Humanities (NEH) Division of Education programs. It also describes an exemplary writing and literature project for high school teachers that the endowment recently funded. In discussing the grant categories within this program, I draw extensively from the Division of Education guidelines. Where appropriate, I include examples of possible projects directly after the discussion of the particular grant category. I also describe an actual project, Writing about Literature: An Institute for High School Teachers, conducted by Elisa Guralnick and Paul Levitt of the University of Colorado, Boulder.

Objectives

The goals of the Humanities Instruction in Elementary and Secondary Schools Program are to increase the effectiveness with which the humanities are taught at all precollege levels, principally through deepening the knowledge and understanding of teachers and administrators, and to improve significantly the working relations among schools, school systems, and colleges and universities. Over the past three years the endowment has given the highest priority to strengthening precollege education. Convinced that it is important to enhance not only teachers' knowledge of the humanities but also the intellectual skills that effective studies of the humanities impart—reasoning, analysis, coherent oral and written expression—the program supports projects designed to accomplish this end. The following four grant categories are part of this program: Independent Study in the Humanities, Preparation of Teachers in the Humanities, Collaborative Projects, and Institutes for Teachers and Administrators.

In all but one grant category (Independent Study in the Humanities), applicants must be individual schools, school systems, colleges, universities, or groups of faculty members at different institutions that prepare proposals collaboratively—that is, the university or college must work closely with the school or schools in developing the NEH application. This joint relationship is critically important to the successful review of an application.

With the exception of Independent Study in the Humanities, applications to the Humanities Instruction in Elementary and Secondary Schools Program are reviewed by NEH staff, panels whose membership reflects the variety in humanities teaching and administration in the nation's schools and colleges, and the National Council on the Humanities (a twenty-six-member committee appointed by the president of the United States to advise the chairman of the endowment). Occasionally, outside reviewers, experts in a subject area, are asked to review applications.

Each application is judged according to several specific criteria: (1) it must be conceptually sound; (2) it must contribute effectively to the participant's knowledge of the subject and his or her ability to teach it; (3) it must contribute to the academic rigor of the regular curriculum; (4) it must involve classroom teachers and administrators in the development and implementation of the proposed project; (5) it must include follow-up activities that will sustain intellectual and pedagogical exchange among college and school personnel; (6) it must provide evidence that the new relationships between the school and the college are likely to continue after project funding ends; (7) the plans for selecting the participants must serve the purposes of the project; (8) it must include plans for dissemination and evaluation; and (9) it must exhibit a strong potential for success. After the applications have been reviewed by staff, panelists, the National Council on the Humanities, and, where necessary, outside reviewers, the chairman of the endowment makes the final decision on each application.

Independent Study in the Humanities

Supported by the NEH through a grant to the Council for Basic Education, the Independent Study in the Humanities program differs from the regular grant categories in the Humanities Instruction in Elementary and Secondary Schools Program. It provides summer fellowships that enable high school teachers with at least five years' experience to further their knowledge of their subjects through two months of independent study in one of the disciplines of the humanities. Any interested high school teacher with the requisite experience is encouraged to submit an application to the Council for Basic Education. The application must outline a work plan of study in the teacher's discipline of the humanities.

Applications are reviewed in two phases. First, a panel of external reviewers selected by the Council for Basic Education reviews each application for competitiveness and quality. If the application is highly rated, it is eligible to compete in the second phase of the competition: a review panel convened in Washington, DC, to discuss the individual and relative merits of the applications and present the best applications to the Council for Basic Education.

In 1983, the first year of the program, 950 high school teachers applied for fellowships and 98 awards of $3,000 each were made. In 1984, 1,000 applications were submitted for review and 118 awards were made. (For additional information about this program, teachers should write to Independent Study in the Humanities, Council for Basic Education, 725 15th St., NW, Washington, DC 20005.)

Improving the Preparation of Teachers in the Humanities: A Special Initiative

The NEH will support the efforts of institutions of higher education to improve programs preparing humanities teachers in elementary and secondary schools. This special initiative goes beyond the endowment's programs for teachers already established in their careers and seeks to strengthen the intellectual base of preservice education in the humanities and to increase the effectiveness of humanities instruction by beginning teachers. The initiative is grounded in the endowment's conviction that the beginning teacher should possess a sound general education and a solid understanding of the major ideas, texts, topics, and issues comprised in the academic disciplines from which the school curriculum is derived. Although the teacher must also be effective in working with young people, the teacher must master subject content along with pedagogical method. A wide range of projects may be proposed. To be successful, however, an applicant must demonstrate that the proposed project will enable new and prospective teachers to deepen their knowledge of the humanities and to acquire skills that will lead to more effective performance in the classroom. Moreover, an applicant should detail, where appropriate, how the project will bring together humanities scholars, teacher educators, experienced school teachers, and school administrators in genuinely collaborative and sustained activities.

Each application should document that the appropriate state education agency supports the goals of the project and will help attain them. This support means, among other things, that prospective teachers who successfully participate in the project and who satisfy all the institution's requirements will be eligible for certification.

Example of a project to improve the preparation of humanities teachers: A college English department arranges with six nearby school districts to work with outstanding language arts teachers from those districts and students at the college who plan to become language arts teachers. The plan is to provide bimonthly seminars and a two-week summer workshop that will give both students and teachers an opportunity for detailed study of major works of English and American literature as well as intensive training in the teaching of expository writing. Education majors who intend to become language arts teachers participate in the project activities after they have completed their practice teaching, which will occur a year earlier than in the past. The district superintendents and the state commissioner all pledge that graduates of this program will be given high priority when teaching positions are filled.

Collaborative Projects

Collaborative projects are designed to assist groups of elementary or secondary school teachers who, as representatives of their schools, wish to establish a systematic and sustained relationship with neighboring colleges or universities to improve the teaching of the humanities in the schools. Discussions with a wide range of educators, superintendents, principals, schoolteachers, university presidents, deans, and faculty members have convinced the endowment that these interinstitutional collaborations, while difficult for schools and colleges or universities to initiate, will, if properly planned and implemented, contribute to the improvement of humanities instruction in the schools. At the same time, they will encourage and foster an important link between two natural resources— the school and the college or university. A major part of the collaborative effort is the expectation that schools and colleges will develop activities and ongoing dialogues that will improve schoolteachers' knowledge and understanding of the subjects they teach as well as enhance college teachers' knowledge and understanding of the problems and achievements of their counterparts in the schools.

All collaborative projects involve summer institutes for teachers and follow-up activities during the succeeding academic year. Summer activities must focus on the serious study of humanities texts, topics, and issues; and follow-up activities must engage the teachers and administrators and the university personnel in a wide range of instructional activities: curriculum development, classroom visitations, guest lectures (by college and high school faculty), study seminars, and other activities appropriate to the individual projects.

To ensure that these projects are carefully planned and that formal links between the school and the college or university are established, the endowment provides a modest amount of planning-grant money to support planning meetings, the development of syllabi and bibliographies, and other activities that will enhance the quality and content of the project. While a planning grant indicates confidence in the applicant's ability to establish a strong collaborative arrangement, it does not guarantee that a full collaborative project will be funded. Therefore, a planning-grant proposal must demonstrate intrinsic value independent of a subsequent request for funds.

Example of a collaborative project: Scholars from a state university and teachers, principals, and the superintendent from a large neighboring school district develop a joint program to improve the schools' secondary literature and history courses. With funding from the school system, the university, a community foundation, and the endowment, history and English faculty members from the university work with high school teachers to design a two-year project for all history and literature teachers in the school system. During the summers, teachers attend an institute on the reform impulse in American society and complementary themes in American fiction from the nineteenth century to the present. The format incorporates practice in expository writing for the participants. During the school year, the teachers and scholars meet twice a month to pursue individual study topics, and members of the university faculty give guest lectures as a regular part of the schools' classroom activities. Project results are disseminated throughout the state through professional journals and conferences. At the same time, the school district and university commit themselves to continuing the program for at least three years after NEH support ends.

Institutes for Teachers and Administrators

Institutes for teachers and administrators generally provide a minimum of four weeks of intensive, residential summer study and appropriate academic-year follow-up activities for groups of humanities teachers or administrators. (Principals' institutes, a special initiative to encourage principals to study humanities texts and topics under the guidance of university professors, may limit summer-study activities to as short a period as three weeks.) Institutes, whether for teachers or for principals, must focus on important texts and ideas in the humanities and the most effective ways of teaching them. While all institutes are conducted by college or university faculty members, master teachers from the schools lead the methods section of the institutes. Both the schools and the host institution should agree to implement plans developed by the teachers during the institute. An application to conduct an institute should describe in detail the plan for selecting participants. The schools that employ the participating teachers are required to endorse the project.

Institutes consist of approximately sixty participants. Depending on the purpose of the program, an institute may be state-based, regional, or national. While institutes vary, the basic format consists of plenary sessions, small group discussions, and afternoon sessions on pedagogy and methods. The plenary sessions bring the faculty members and the participants together to establish the context and content of the day's discussion. The small-group sessions allow an institute faculty member to meet with approximately fifteen participants to work through the text, discussing a variety of humanities topics and issues. And since participants need an opportunity to consider ways of applying their new learning in their classrooms, the afternoon sessions give teachers and master teachers an opportunity to concentrate on questions of pedagogy and methods. In addition, applicants are urged to plan time for independent study, cultural visitations, and library work.

One of the central parts of any project to improve humanities instruction is the opportunity that participants are afforded to improve their writing. And while the endowment no longer emphasizes writing institutes as a means of improving participants' writing skills, it does encourage applicants, no matter what their humanities discipline, to engage participants in regular writing activities that link the study of the humanities to the principles of clear, effective exposition. Thus, not only literature institutes but history, foreign language, and classics institutes should include significant writing components within the context of textual analysis. This content-oriented approach to the central discipline of the humanities offers participants an important way both to strengthen their knowledge in a subject discipline and to improve their writing skills.

Example of an institute for teachers and administrators (based on an NEH-supported project): In June 1983, two professors from the Department of English at the University of Colorado, Boulder, Elisa Guralnick and Paul Levitt, submitted an application to the Humanities Instruction in Elementary and Secondary Schools Program to establish a statewide institute for sixty high school teachers to study writing through the examination of literature. The major premise underlying the proposal was the professors' belief that students cannot be expected to write clearly and gracefully about the humanities or to understand the critical importance of the humanities unless their teachers have been adequately trained both in writing and in interpreting literary texts. Thus, the applicants proposed a summer institute and follow-up activities that would teach the skills of description and argument, using selected classic texts as subject matter—texts that give voice to recurring themes in western civilization. The texts included works on the state's list of required high school readings as well as works that high school teachers rarely have the background to teach with authority. The following is an overview of the reading list:

Style (Week 1):
Thucydides, *The Peloponnesian War*: from book 2, "Pericles' Funeral Oration"

and "The Plague (in Athens)" ; from the end of book 5, "The Melian Dialogue"; and from the start of book 6, "The Debate at Syracuse"
Edward Gibbon, *The Decline and Fall of the Roman Empire*: chapter 15, "The Progress of the Christian Religion"; chapter 16, "The Conduct of the Roman Government toward the Christians"

Form (Week 2):
Sophocles, *Oedipus Rex*
Sigmund Freud, *A General Introduction to Psychoanalysis*: part 3; and "Mourning and Melancholia," from *The Collected Papers of Sigmund Freud*, vol. 4

Content (Week 3):
Plato, *Apology, Crito*, and *Phaedo*
Xenophon, *Apology*
T. S. Eliot, *Murder in the Cathedral*
Robert Bolt, *A Man for All Seasons*

Composite (Week 4):
Homer, *The Odyssey*
Mark Twain, *The Adventures of Huckleberry Finn*

The applicants felt that the categories used to organize the weekly reading list—style, form, and content—would be particularly useful in a literature and writing institute because they concern aesthetic questions: namely, which words to put in which places to fashion a style; which parts to organize in which order to shape a coherent form; and which meanings to develop or treat in which ways to delight and instruct.

In explaining the intellectual rationale for the readings, the applicants said:

> For the purpose of discussing style (week one), we have selected Thucydides and Gibbon, because in both there is a particular view of human existence—cynical, realistic, disdainful of cant and hypocrisy—that is rendered ironically. As irony is one of the most difficult techniques to master in writing, the teachers should profit from close analysis of Thucydides' and Gibbon's prose. Both authors assume that all people share a desire for power, for material gain, and for pleasure—a desire people might sometimes be able to control through the exercise of reason, but one that all too often persists, despite idealism and good intentions. Since true wisdom resides in seeing the world as it is, not as it pretends to be, it is those who decline to disabuse themselves of dreams and delusions, who let themselves be misled by the idle speculation of poets or priests, who are untrue to their own natures, that Thucydides and Gibbon ironically censure.
>
> In the readings from Thucydides, the first selection in each pair praises people for having values and standards that the second selection ridicules people for having forgot. Hence the Athenians' behavior with respect to their burial customs, for instance, is praised in "Pericles' Funeral Oration" and condemned in "The Plague." In addition to observing how Thucydides shapes his prose to express his censure, the teachers can learn, from each pair, how the juxtaposition of descriptive passages can form the basis of an argument.
>
> In the chapters from Edward Gibbon, in which the historian traces the early

progress of Christianity and the Roman government's policy toward the Christians, sex and Christianity provide Gibbon with ample opportunity to display his ironic wit—a wit that is worth studying not just for what can be learned about polemical style, but for other reasons as well. Irony distances Gibbon from his subject matter, and thus lends him the appearance of detachment from his history; it provides him with a protective device in an age when explicit attacks on Christianity laid a writer open to prosecution and penalties under the statutes of the realm; it enables him to steer a course between a humorous and objective view of history; it lets him evade judgments that he does not wish to make; and it allows him to express his natural playfulness and gaity. By contrast, the inexperienced writer attempts to gain distance by using the passive voice, attempts to create a protective device by being vague, attempts to be evenhanded by adopting shifting points of view, attempts to evade judgment by endlessly qualifying a point, and attempts to be playful and gay by forging a self-conscious humor. Gibbon can serve as a corrective for such errors while demonstrating the multiple uses of irony.

In week two, for our discussion of form, we have chosen *Oedipus Rex* and several of Freud's essays in order to show the relationship between analytic exposition in drama and psychoanalytic method. Both analytic exposition and psychoanalytic method are expressions of [the human] impulse to tell stories; and as all storytellers know, the point at which a writer commences [a] narrative invokes a logic that dictates the form of the piece. Permit us to explain.

The function of dramatic exposition is, of course, to put an audience in possession of antecedent facts necessary to an understanding of the situation at the start of a play. When an exposition is conventional, it may be formal, as in a prologue, or it may be dramatized. Moreover, it may acquaint the audience with only a part of the antecedent material, or with the whole of it; that is, the audience may be given information in advance of the characters in the play, and then enjoy seeing the characters discover what the audience already knows; or the audience may discover a part of the information along with the characters. Finally, the audience may be told nothing at all in advance, in which case they become, as it were, innocent bystanders, gathering information by bits and shreds, forming their opinion by what they see and hear, learning along with the characters and not in advance of them.

When an exposition is analytic—that is, when the action of a play begins immediately before the crisis and is then propelled forward by a revelation of the past and a discussion of its effect on the present—the exposition is dramatized. The analytic exposition may be employed for the purpose of condensing a long story within the bounds of space and time (*Oedipus*); or it may be used to show the effects of the past on the present (*Oedipus, Ghosts, All My Sons*), or to show evolution or change in character (*A Doll House, Death of a Salesman*). The main function of the analytic exposition, then, is to reflect the past in the present and to show how the present results from the past.

The same is true of the psychoanalytic method or form. Psychoanalysts assume that there is a causal relationship between past and present. The progressive revealing of the past is intended to show how past experiences influence present behavior. The patient's story of his past is analyzed and, in the process, his character explained. Freud, of course, is the most famous practitioner of the method, even if not its true founder. And the best descriptions of Freudian psychoanalysis are the lectures in *The General Introduction to Psychoanalysis*, part three, and the essay "Mourning and Melancholia" in volume four of *The Collected Papers of Sigmund Freud*.

A comparative study of analytic exposition in drama and the form of psychoanalysis will be illuminating to teachers of writing because it vividly demon strates how the choice of an opening sentence or paragraph determines the form of all that comes after. It also reveals that the very activities of literary analysis and writing about literature rest in great part on procedures analogous to the psychoanalytic method, as the critic is expected to identify and interpret elements that explain the nature of the text.

In week three, we turn to content, having selected as our texts Plato's and Xenophon's stories of the trial of Socrates. In addition to the obvious comparison, which can provoke a splendid discussion of how content determines form (why does the author select this form and not another to present this incident? to what effect? to achieve what end?), both works raise the universal thematic issue of individual conscience versus the needs of the state. To give historical breadth to the issue, we have selected two modern plays that take for their settings the Middle Ages and Renaissance England. That modern writers use historical settings not only to distance an issue, but also to suggest its currency, should help teachers illustrate to students who say they have nothing to write about—students who think that nothing is relevant unless it is modern—that, as the Psalmist says, "there is no new thing under the sun" and consequently no humanistic idea is not both ancient and modern.

Finally, in week four, in order to unite the issues of style, form, and content, we plan to discuss all of these categories in conjunction with Homer's *Odyssey* and Twain's *Huckleberry Finn*, two works that lend themselves to a variety of comparative studies. Both are narratives, both are adventures, and both are travel literature. Both stories are framed by an outer story, both are episodic in form, and both depend on hyperbole and exaggeration for their stylistic effects, no doubt because Odysseus and Huck are great liars and storytellers. Although Odysseus is an epic hero and a soldier while Huck is a picaresque hero and a runaway, both characters experience a series of trials and temptations, both define themselves through these experiences, and both are ultimately looking for a home. Hence the two works will enable us to integrate the subjects of the first three weeks and so to arrive at a fuller understanding of why, in matters of writing as well as of architecture, "form," as Louis Sullivan observed, "ever follows function." A teacher or a student who can understand this point can also understand that papers can never be graded for content, because content is inseparable from style.

In 1984 the University of Colorado, Boulder, devoted a four-week summer institute for high school teachers to the topic Writing about Literature. Teachers were required to write daily and to scrutinize one another's writing in seminars that consisted of groups of seven participants working with one university faculty member. Instruction in the seminars proceeded from analysis of the teachers' own writing and required that the teachers revise their work not once but several times until the papers were polished. The schedule called for each university faculty member to (1) deliver 3 lectures on texts from the reading list; (2) lead 60 hours of writing seminars (15 hours a week); (3) grade 285 writing assignments (15 a day for 19 days); (4) conduct 22½ hours of individual conferences with the participants (7½ hours a week for each of the 3 weeks); (5) consult with guest lecturers (national experts in writing) for 8 hours (2 hours with each expert); and (6) attend films, plays, and other institute activities. The staff of the institute consisted of the codirectors, Elisa Guralnick and Paul Levitt, three university faculty members, two master teachers, and four national experts in writing.

The participating high school teachers were chosen by a steering committee composed of the institute's faculty and administrators and teachers from the Boulder and Denver communities. In selecting the participants, the committee gave preference to teachers who (1) were employed full-time or part-time in the teaching of English or language arts in a public or private Colorado high school; (2) had letters of endorsement from their principals, guaranteeing them the opportunity to teach at least two courses in composition or advanced placement English during the year following the institute; (3) completed application forms, including statements of commitment to read the works on the reading list before the start of the institute, to complete the course work in the institute, to complete all follow-up assignments, and to participate in the required follow-up activities; (4) submitted, as part of their applications, three-page argumentative papers on pre-announced topics; and (5) could verify the willingness of their home institutions to give them released time to prepare for and participate in the institute's follow-up activities. The follow-up activities to the Writing about Literature institute took place between October 1984 and May 1985. While these activities focused on the institute participants, they were designed to transmit the institute's program to a large number of noninstitute participants.

Each institute participant was required to submit four papers for evaluation and to participate in at least three of the following activities:

Regional conferences. During the academic year the faculty organized five two-day regional conferences. The conferences were of two types. One type proceeded under the assumption that a significant number of participants were teachers who attended the 1984 institute. Activities focused on intensive study of new texts identified by the teachers themselves as important to their curricula. The conference reflected the focus of the institute, with sessions devoted to form, content, style, and methods. Participants completed preconference reading assignments before attending the conference.

A second type of regional conference was designed as an introduction to the work of the institute. Institute staff and a small number of previous participants made presentations based on the work of the 1984 institute. In all cases, regional conferences were open to noninstitute participants.

One-day conferences. Another type of conference, designed for teachers within easy commuting distance, was a one-day event organized around narrowly focused study topics identified by faculty and participants during the summer. As in the regional conferences, participants arrived at a one-day conference having read assigned material and, in some cases, having written papers. Six one-day conferences took place during the academic year.

Residencies by institute staff. The institute's faculty members spent as many as sixty days in residencies in high schools throughout the state. Residencies included meeting with both groups of teachers and individual teachers, as well as with their classes, and also gave the institute faculty members and teachers an opportunity to review curriculum materials and to discuss strategies, ideas, and reading lists developed in the institute program.

At the end of this one-year project, many high school literature teachers in the state of Colorado better understood that literary style is a vehicle of meaning; that form creates meaning; that familiar themes recur through the literature of disparate periods and countries, obliterating historical and geographical distance, so that all great works of art become both timeless and universal; that teachers need not be daunted by great works of literature, need not worry whether students will find them relevant, since these works are all ideal models of how to forge meaning out of minute particulars; and that literary analysis is a tool for interpreting not only literature and other written documents but the spoken word as well. Participants in the institute also emerged with a deeper appreciation of classical texts and a better understanding of how to transmit that appreciation to their students. In reviewing the Writing about Literature project, the staff, the panel, and the members of the National Council on the Humanities concluded that the proposal significantly improved the teaching of sixty Colorado high school literature teachers, thereby indirectly benefiting hundreds, if not thousands, of students who will study with these teachers.

One aim of the endowment's Humanities Instruction in Elementary and Secondary Schools Program is to encourage projects such as the Colorado, Boulder, project. This project, like more than one hundred current NEH-supported precollegiate projects in the humanities, is an excellent example of academic rigor, intellectual depth, clarity of purpose, and the collaboration of university personnel and schoolteachers and administrators.

For additional information about the Humanities Instruction in Elementary and Secondary Schools Program, individuals may write to Division of Education Programs, Room 302, The National Endowment for the Humanities, 1100 Pennsylvania Ave., NW, Washington, DC 20506.

Editor's Note

This essay not only describes a specific school-college collaborative project in writing and literature but also outlines a range of funding programs concerned with school-college cooperation to which schools interested in initiating or extending their own projects can apply for support.

University of Illinois, Urbana-Champaign: University Associates in Rhetoric Program

R. Baird Shuman

The University Associates in Rhetoric Program was born one day late in February 1978 when the Rhetoric Advisory Committee, of which I was a member, addressed the question of how to staff the nearly three hundred sections of freshman English that the University of Illinois, Urbana-Champaign, offers in a typical year. Our own English graduate students normally could cover one-half to two-thirds of these sections, but the remaining classes usually were covered by graduate students from other departments or by adjuncts with backgrounds in English.

Background

The Rhetoric Advisory Committee was asked to consider other ways to staff our freshman offerings, and I mused that we might do well to consider initiating a program that would allow experienced secondary school teachers of English to come to the university for a year to teach for us and to take courses. I suggested that we might publicize such a program nationally and find teachers whose school districts would be willing to give them paid sabbatical leaves while they participated in the program. Because the full year's leave would normally carry half pay, I recommended that we pay the other half, so that those coming to us would not do so at a smaller salary than they would have received had they remained at home.

Arnold Tibbetts, who was then director of freshman rhetoric, expressed considerable interest in the suggestion, and Keneth Kinnamon, head of the Department of English, asked me to put my ideas in writing. I did so that very afternoon, stipulating that, to be eligible, applicants must have taught successfully for six or more years and hold at least a master's degree in English or in English education. They would also have to meet the entrance requirements for graduate study in English at the university because they would be taking classes, although they would not be degree candidates.

Kinnamon acted on my proposal immediately and passed it on to the director of the School of Humanities, who, within forty-eight hours, authorized us to proceed at once with the program. We agreed that each associate would be paid a minimum of $9,000 a year to teach a total of six classes, three each semester. Our maximum compensation at that time was fixed at $10,000, although we now pay all associates at the top of our pay scale for graduate assistants, about $12,000 a year.

I was taken quite by surprise when the program was approved so swiftly, and I had serious doubts that, given the lateness of our beginning, we would be able to find a pool of applicants for the 1978–79 academic year. I was asked to coordinate the program and was given authority to bring up to ten associates into the university.

Through the cooperation of our good and dependable neighbor, the National Council of Teachers of English (NCTE), I was able to obtain a mailing list of superintendents of school districts in the United States and its possessions. I quickly prepared descriptive material about the program, and within a week approximately a thousand packets were sent to superintendents.

To my amazement, despite the short notice, we had twenty-two applicants for the coming academic year, and from this field we admitted six. Although two of these six had to defer coming until the following year, our first four associates were with us when school opened in the fall. My colleagues were apprehensive that three sections of freshman English would prove a crushing burden, but I knew enough about high school teaching loads to realize that, while the university job would not be easy, the people we had admitted could manage it. At the university, they would teach no more than sixty-six students each semester and would be spared the extracurricular duties that are typically thrust on high school teachers. And, best of all, they had their choice of teaching a two-day or a three-day week.

Objectives

The department's initial objective in instituting this program was to find competent and experienced English professionals to cover classes that had to be taught, but we also had significant objectives in mind for the associates who came into the program. We viewed this new offering as a further step in the university's articulation with secondary English teachers, which began in 1908 when the university sponsored an English teachers' association, out of which eventually grew the National Council of Teachers of English. Since 1908, the university has had a close tie with English teachers' organizations, and the university now serves as headquarters for the Illinois Association of Teachers of English. The department provides released time to the executive secretary of this organization and to the editor of its quarterly journal, the *Illinois English Bulletin*. The department also sponsors an articulation conference for secondary English teachers every year.

It was our belief that carefully selected teachers coming into the University Associates in Rhetoric Program from every corner of the United States would learn a great deal from one another about various approaches to teaching English. The university would provide them with an intellectually stimulating environment and with unsurpassed research facilities. The cultural offerings of the university's Krannert Center and of other local facilities such as the NCTE headquarters would provide another facet to what the associates might gain from being with us.

In the one required course, participants would be exposed to recent developments in rhetorical theory, and this exposure would be buttressed by their teaching experiences. We felt that we had the perfect environment for intermeshing the theoretical with the practical. Associates were also encouraged to take additional courses in areas of interest to them and to work with faculty members in preparing materials for publication if they wished to do so.

Certainly a salient objective has been to give secondary school English teachers a realistic view of the current demands that major universities place on their students in writing programs. If the program served no purpose other than to send teachers back to their districts better able to help college-bound students prepare for the actualities of college writing and higher-level reasoning, the experience would have been worthwhile.

We also hoped that those who came to us would return to their home districts better equipped to bring about any needed change in their English curricula. Many home districts rely on returning associates as resource people in curriculum development.

One of our goals was to have a broad geographical representation among the associates so that all the participants would gain some insights into how English is taught in various regions as well as in a variety of socioeconomic situations. Over the years this objective has been met quite well. At this writing, we have attracted a total of thirty-two participants from nineteen states and the District of Columbia, with seven states contributing two or more associates: California (2), Colorado, District of Columbia, Hawaii, Idaho, Illinois (6), Indiana, Mississippi, Nebraska, New Hampshire, New Jersey, New Mexico, New York (2), Pennsylvania (2), South Carolina (2), South Dakota, Utah, Virginia, Washington (2), and Wisconsin (3). Usually when we have had an associate from a given state, applications from that state have increased in following years.

Structure and Procedures

Because we hope to provide a link between the theoretical and the practical, the program is designed so that the freshman classes the associates teach provide a laboratory in which the instructors attempt to apply what they are learning in class and through weekly meetings with their rhetoric advisers.

The program begins with an intensive orientation that occupies about four days immediately before the beginning of classes. In this orientation, all our new instructors are introduced to the freshman rhetoric program, to the facilities available to them from the rhetoric office, to the textbooks, and to the standards of grading generally followed in the freshman classes. Participants in the orientation sessions will already have had their textbooks for two to three months and will have received copies of the quite extensive instructor's manual that the director of freshman rhetoric has prepared. During the orientation, participants meet their rhetoric advisers, seasoned instructors who are given released time to work with six or seven of the new instructors for their entire first year of teaching in the program. All advisers hold weekly meetings with their advisory groups, observe and confer with new instructors, and make themselves readily accessible to those in their groups.

Each associate is expected to enroll in the Professional Seminar in Writing, a course taught in the fall semester of each year by the director of freshman rhetoric. This course directs attention to recent developments in rhetorical theory. Each student is expected to do individual research on topics related to rhetoric, to produce two papers in the course of the semester, and to prepare an extended oral report on one of these papers for classroom presentation.

The associates in the seminar are encouraged to focus their papers in such a way that publication might be a reasonable outcome. The results have been gratifying, and a number of associates have succeeded in publishing their papers in professional journals. Nearly all associates go far beyond the minimum requirements of the professional seminar, producing quite exhaustive papers of close to publishable quality. Some associates have taken independent studies with the director of the program during the spring semester in order to work on honing their papers for submission to appropriate journals.

Each group of associates has established its own social milieu, and out of this have grown frequent and valuable learning experiences. Theater parties, potluck suppers, and other such activities have brought the group together with faculty members in informal, loosely structured settings conducive to good discussion and fruitful interchange.

Most of the associates, who are granted free tuition, elect while they are in the program to take courses in addition to the Professional Seminar in Writing. The range of courses they have taken has been extensive, although the current emphasis seems to be on computer programming.

Problems

The University Associates in Rhetoric Program has had its troubles. When it was initiated, free tuition was not available to participants, although each was permitted to register for courses at the in-state tuition rate. This problem has now been overcome.

The program would be a stronger training program if funding were available to reduce the teaching load to two courses a semester. It would also be highly desirable to have participants come to campus for an intensive instructional program in modern grammar, including dialectology, for two weeks before orientation, but no funding is presently available for such a program, which would require a stipend for each associate as well as faculty salaries for those administering and instructing in the program.

No released time has been granted to the coordinator of the program, but this problem is not serious, because the coordinator receives released time for serving as director of freshman rhetoric and can administer the program as a part of the freshman program.

The most significant initial problem came from English graduate students who feared that their employment might be threatened by the associates. This problem no longer exists because it is clear that, despite the presence of the associates, we have sufficient work for all our own graduate students as well as for substantial numbers from other departments. Graduate students have been far more cordial toward recent associates than toward earlier ones. The associates are now included routinely in social events planned by graduate students and participate fully in the social and intellectual life of the department.

Housing problems have never been great, because Urbana-Champaign has a good variety of rentals, but we now have established a network in which associates from a given year correspond with incoming associates about housing and other practical concerns. The university's housing for married students is also open to married associates, a number of whom have availed themselves of this convenience. Even the associate who arrived with his wife and six children found accommodations quite readily.

We initially feared that those who came into the program might not wish to return to their home districts. However, some twenty-five of the thirty-two associates we have had are back on the job in the districts from which they came. One has retired as a schoolteacher and is currently teaching freshman composition in a college near his home. Five are now engaged in doctoral studies, but of these, two are back in their home districts and are pursuing their studies part-time, one is in another secondary school situation, one has returned to the University of Illinois to pursue the doctorate, and one is still in the associates' program and will not return to her district next year. Only two former associates have left teaching (aside from the one retiree), but they are working in positions closely related to the profession.

Plans

The University Associates in Rhetoric Program is now operating successfully and we expect to continue it as long as the university needs to hire people other than its own graduate students to teach freshman English. Although our need is not likely to be great enough to justify bringing in the ten associates we were originally authorized to admit, we will probably have four to six people in the program each year.

Because many school districts do not grant sabbatical leaves, we no longer require the assurance of such leaves before we admit applicants, although we strongly urge districts to provide some support to their teachers who are in this training program. Since this requirement has been changed, a few teachers have come to the program with no support from the home district, but most still receive some support.

Funding and Staffing

University funding for this program has come from the English department's budget and has involved no costs beyond what would be involved in having the classes taught by other personnel. The only other items charged to the department's budget are postage and the occasional long-distance telephone calls associated with the program. Because the associates are well qualified by both training and experience, we feel that the cost of running the program is justifiable.

No extraordinary staffing is required for the University Associates in Rhetoric Program. The director of freshman rhetoric coordinates the program as part of his or her normal duties. The rhetoric advisers carry associates as part of their normal advising load.

Recommendations

A program of this sort is most effective if it draws teachers from a broad geographical area. The interchange that this distribution encourages is of utmost value to participants. Our associates have been diverse in other ways, although we have not consciously striven to make them so. They have ranged in age, for example, from twenty-nine to sixty-seven, with the average participant being between thirty and fifty. We have achieved a reasonable balance between male and female participants in each year's group, although this too was by accident rather than by design (see Table 1).

Because it is vital that those coming into a program of this sort hold their own with the department's regular graduate students, admissions standards must be strenuous. Once participants are on campus, it is desirable to give them as many opportunities as possible to interact with other teachers from the state. We involve our associates actively as presenters in our annual Articulation Conference for Secondary School English Teachers as well as in our Community College Articulation Conference. We encourage them to be active in the Illinois Association of Teachers of English and to attend its meetings. Because the National Council of Teachers of English is a unique resource in the Urbana-Champaign area, we provide opportunities for the associates to visit the national headquarters and to become acquainted with those who administer that organization, as well as to learn how to use such NCTE facilities as the ERIC materials.

Two distinct benefits of the University Associates in Rhetoric Program are that it is field-based and that it extends over a full year. Participants thus have an opportunity in the second semester of the program to introduce the techniques and strategies they have learned through their course work during the first semester and to improve some of the teaching methodologies they developed with the first three classes. Because the associates learn theory that can be applied immediately in their classroom teaching, the program provides a dimension not available to those who study theory in isolation from teaching.

The University Associates in Rhetoric Program has made me realize that a university serves teachers best when it works with them over extended periods. The teachers who complete the program can go back to their home districts and reach dozens of other teachers in their own schools and in their professional organizations. Their students also benefit, because the associates return to their districts refreshed and revitalized by the experience the program provides.

Table 1
Sex and Age Distribution of Associates

Age:	Under 30	30-39	40-49	50-59	Over 60	Total
Men	1	10	3	0	1	15
Women	0	3	8	4	2	17
Total:	1	13	11	4	3	32

University of Michigan: The Outreach Program of the English Composition Board

Jay L. Robinson and Patricia L. Stock

Designed initially as support for the University of Michigan's own writing program, the Outreach Program of the English Composition Board quickly extended its aims and scope in response to external demands. At the outset, the program's aims were to inform feeder high schools and community colleges of the expectations embedded in the requirements of the university's new writing program and to assist faculty members in the schools and colleges to develop programs and instructional methods that would prepare their students to meet these expectations. The program, however, soon attracted attention from teachers and planners outside the state of Michigan.

Background

Because deficiencies in writing and reading constitute a national problem, and because the country has become increasingly aware that widespread advanced literacy is vital to its economic and social well-being, the directors of Michigan's outreach program found themselves deluged with requests to extend the reach of the program beyond the state's boundaries. In the deluge swirled both promise and opportunity, but also the possibility of drowning.

A brief history may help illuminate both potential and peril. In 1973 and 1974, the College of Literature, Science, and the Arts at the University of Michigan conducted an internal review of its graduation requirements, the first such review since the 1940s. During open hearings, students and faculty members expressed opinions not only about how adequately the college prepared students for advanced study or the world of work but also about the adequacy of students' preuniversity preparation for the college's graduation requirements.

One recurrent theme in the testimony of students and faculty members alike was dissatisfaction with the quality of students' literacy both on entering the college and on leaving.

Responding to this testimony, the college established the English Composition Board (ECB), composed of faculty members from across the disciplines, which in turn developed a new graduation requirement in writing.

Structure

The new requirement took shape as a seven-part program, with six parts within the college and one extending beyond its confines. Those within the college are the *placement essay*, required of all incoming undergraduates; *tutorial instruction*, required of all students whose performance on the placement essay demonstrates the need for such assistance; *introductory composition*, required of most students to make them more proficient writers; the *writing workshop*, available to any student seeking support; *junior-senior-level writing courses*, offered and required primarily in students' areas of concentration; and *research* into the effectiveness of all parts of the program.

The seventh part of the program reaches outside the college and includes five types of activities that relate the teaching of writing in secondary schools and community colleges to the writing program at the university: *writing conferences*, intended primarily to inform preuniversity teachers of both the English Composition Board's program of instruction and its ability and willingness to engage in outreach projects; *one- and two-day seminars*—conducted in secondary schools, community colleges, and universities throughout Michigan and elsewhere—fostering discussions with teachers about the current state of theory and practice in the art of teaching writing at all levels; *writing workshops*, held at the University of Michigan and designed to provide teachers with intensive work in the teaching of writing; extended *curriculum and staff development projects*, undertaken with a few school districts requesting such service; and publication of *fforum*, a journal providing teachers of writing with a vehicle for mutual instruction.

Funded by the Andrew W. Mellon Foundation, the University of Michigan, and private donors, the outreach program was initiated to fulfill the English Composition Board's promise to the faculty of the College of Literature, Science, and the Arts to support improvement of writing instruction in the schools and colleges that send students to the university. In agreeing to play an expanded role in the teaching of writing, Michigan faculty members recognized that they were not only committing scarce resources to instruction that some considered the responsibility of preparatory education but increasing their own work load. Quite properly, they demanded concomitant commitments from teachers in feeder schools. The more experienced writing teachers on the university faculty recognized that without complementary and cooperative instructional programs in preparatory schools and colleges, Michigan's own writing program was more likely to fail. Learning to write well requires effort and instruction throughout a student's education.

In May 1978 the English Composition Board launched its outreach effort by inviting teachers and administrators from every high school, community college, and four-year college in Michigan and Northern Ohio to come to Ann Arbor to discuss the college's new writing program and to consider the board's offer to provide seminars in the teaching of writing to the faculties of schools that might request them. About 250 schools sent 550 representatives to this conference. The following December (1978) 350 teachers and administrators who had attended the May conference and expressed interest in the outreach program were invited to a second conference to advise the board about not only its proposed seminars for writing teachers but also the shape its internal program should take in relation to students' prior learning.

Following these initial planning conferences, the board conducted, between January 1979 and May 1982, a total of 272 in-service seminars in secondary schools and two- and four-year colleges and two intensive writing workshops.

When held in secondary schools, the seminars usually consisted of a morning spent with a school's entire faculty to discuss the concept of writing across the curriculum and an afternoon spent with English teachers and other teachers of writing. Audiences sometimes included members of school boards or parents from the community. The intensive three-day workshops, held in June 1979 and June 1980, provided opportunities for more careful instruction in theories and methods of composition; each was attended by 150 teachers from Michigan. While teams of two from the university faculty conducted the in-service seminars, the workshops required the participation of about a dozen university faculty members—some from the English department, some from other academic disciplines, and some from the staff of the English Composition Board.

Because schools, colleges, and universities across the United States soon asked the English Composition Board to conduct, or participate in, seminars and conferences on the teaching of writing, the outreach program quickly expanded beyond Michigan's boundaries. More than forty institutions—including Arizona State University; the University of Arizona; Bucknell University; the University of California, Irvine; Howard University; Lehigh University; the University of Nebraska, Lincoln; Ohio University; the University of Southern California; Southern University in New Orleans; the University of Texas, Austin; the University of Utah; the University of Western Carolina; and the University of Wisconsin, Stevens Point—have taken part in this aspect of the board's program. Some institutions have developed writing programs on the model developed at Michigan, and many of these include their own outreach programs.

In June 1981, the board experimented with an expanded and changed version of its summer workshops. With generous funding from the Andrew W. Mellon Foundation, the board offered a three-day conference, Literacy in the '80s. The conference was preceded by one three-day workshop and followed by another—the first for 175 teachers from sixteen states and the District of Columbia, the second for a like number of teachers from Michigan. All 350 teachers attended the conference, making possible a broad exchange of materials and views. Out-of-state participants were organized in groups of university, community college, and secondary school teachers from particular geographical areas (e.g., the New Orleans group included faculty members from Tulane University, Southern University in New Orleans, Xavier University of Louisiana, Eleanor McMain Magnet Secondary School, and O. Perry Walker High School). The aim of this organization was to develop networks of writing teachers in other parts of the country like the one in Michigan.

There were similar intentions behind extended workshops the board sponsored on the topics Writing and Thinking and Reading Student Writing during the summers of 1983 and 1984, respectively. These workshops offered opportunities for extended study to about sixty high school and college teachers each year. Once again, participants organized into groups of high school and college faculty members from selected geographical areas learned from one another, seeking solutions for common problems even as they worked within their own groups to address issues particular to their own settings and locales. We have learned from our summer workshops that groups formed for participation in a workshop often achieve a sense of cohesion that supports cooperative work when individual participants return to their own schools and begin to incorporate new ideas and methods into their teaching. The workshops offer school and college teachers the rare opportunity to study together and to discover that they have similar concerns and problems amenable to common solutions. Building on these workshop experiences, the board has begun to cosponsor workshops with other institutions of higher learning in their geographic regions. In the summer of 1984, workshops were offered in conjunction with Arizona State University; the University of California, Irvine; Southern University of New Orleans; and New York University together with the State University of New York, Albany.

Development of a comprehensive writing program and participation in collaborative work with schools have enabled faculty members at Michigan to perceive more clearly the intellectual challenges involved in trying to determine what literacy is and how it functions, both in the academy and in society. Assistance from the Mellon Foundation enabled the English Composition Board to assemble an advisory committee of scholars from the University of Michigan, the Annenberg School of Communication of the University of Southern California, the Law School of the University of Chicago, and the School of Medicine of the University of Maryland to study the implications that a changing concept of literacy has for liberal education, with special attention to the impact of developing media on the teaching of literacy—topics treated in the 1981 conference, Literacy for the '80s. The committee met on the University of Michigan campus once or twice each month from September 1981 through April 1985. Sometimes individual committee members led seminars for one another (e.g., Rudolf Arnheim, Visual Thinking, 9 Feb. 1983); at other times, invited guests came to the campus to present public lectures, seminars for interested faculty members, and seminars for the committee (e.g., Stephen Toulmin, Rationality and Reason: The Relations of Logic to Method, 7 Oct. 1982).

In the spirit of its outreach program, the English Composition Board makes every effort to keep its colleagues in Michigan and beyond informed of the results of its own studies. In March 1983, for example, on the two days preceding the national meeting in Detroit of the Conference on College Composition and Communication, the board sponsored a two-day workshop, Evolving Literacy and Revolutionary Technology. Invited as special participants in the workshop were some forty influential scholars, directors of writing programs, and writing teachers who carried the issues and topics raised in Ann Arbor to the national conference of teachers of writing. Workshops like this, coupled with publication of *fforum* and of proceedings and special collections of essays, serve as useful media for the dissemination of information relevant to ongoing program planning and curricular change.

Problems

A major problem for the board resulting from its activities is how to balance its responsibilities to the university faculty and to Michigan's schools and teachers with requests for assistance and cooperation from other states. The board's financial resources and the time and energy of its members are limited. It is well known that programs involving school-college cooperation often have short, though sometimes brilliant, histories; they are exceedingly difficult to sustain. The recent past of the English Composition Board's efforts is a history of difficult choices among priorities and institutions. The board is trying to develop models for school-college cooperation that can be embedded and further developed in a variety of settings and to investigate problems and issues in the field of literacy and its uses that are of genuine national concern.

Recommendations

Insofar as Michigan's outreach program has been a successful beginning, it has been so for the following reasons. First, we were able to rely on the good services of able, well-established, and committed faculty members—mainly from the traditional academic disciplines—whose expertise matched their commitment. Second, since our outreach efforts were closely connected to curricular changes within the University of Michigan, we could invite the schools to engage in a cooperative effort, instead of enjoining them to undertake responsibilities we were avoiding. We did not impose tasks on teachers; rather, we asked teachers to collaborate with us. And third, we enjoyed effective and energetic support from our own administration, from the dean of the college to the university president, as well as generous and intelligently allocated financial support from the Mellon Foundation.

The Future

The board is aware that its outreach work has been but a beginning in the challenging task of coordinating instruction in literacy in schools and colleges. Its visits to schools and the conferences and workshops it has conducted have introduced teachers to new ideas and practices and have conveyed a sense of common interest and commitment. Such a beginning must be followed by opportunities for teachers and schools to translate new ideas and newly kindled interest into programs, materials, and practices that meet the demands of their particular situations.

Whether or not Michigan's beginning will lead to a fully developed and sustained program adequate to existing needs is a question that nags us; a positive answer is by no means certain. The number of faculty members at the university who can be usefully involved is regrettably small, and burnout has already caused casualties among them. Furthermore, although several of us have been engaged in on-going research into issues of language learning and assessment with teacher-researchers in several Michigan secondary schools since September 1983, we can no longer maintain the rate of visits to school and college campuses that we managed from 1979 to 1982. The absence of recognition and reward for university faculty members who concern themselves with public secondary education contributes to both burnout and the likelihood of casualties. Possible though partial solutions to these problems include the use of networking, so that no one institution carries the whole burden of cooperative efforts, and exploitation of research potential in the areas of a collaborative effort. Universities must, after all, protect their own priorities, and they are justified in expecting to benefit from their participation in cooperative programs. Funding agencies, whether private or public, must be sensitive to the aims and needs of school and college.

What has Michigan's outreach program accomplished? Less than we would like to be able to claim, and less than we would have claimed before we became fully aware of the problems that demand attention. But we do make some claims: we have given professional support—really ethical support, in the old sense of ethos—to hundreds of teachers, and we consider such support vital to professionals as beleaguered as teachers now are; we have been agents of change in a number of schools now engaged in the improvement of writing programs; we have participated in a modest handful of extensive projects that will result in new curricula; and we have been useful to our colleagues in other universities, in part by offering a model adaptable to other institutional arrangements and in part by demonstrating that university faculty members can be seriously engaged in the teaching and study of literacy. We have only made a beginning, but we are further ahead than when we started.

Note

This essay appeared earlier in a slightly different form in "The Outreach Program of the English Composition Board: An Experiment in University-School Cooperation," *Partners in Education: Excellence through Cooperation*, proc. of a statewide conference, Baton Rouge: Louisiana Dept. of Education, 1983, 13–22. Used with permission.

Table 1
ECB-Sponsored Seminars on the Teaching of Writing, January 1979–May 1982

	Michigan	*Outside Michigan*	*Total*
Secondary school	196	4	200
Community colleges	10	13	23
Colleges and universities	15	34	49
Total	221	51	272

National Endowment for the Humanities: Summer Seminars for Secondary School Teachers

Ronald Herzman

In the summer of 1983, the National Endowment for the Humanities began a new program, Summer Seminars for Secondary School Teachers. Modeled after the successful Summer Seminars for College Teachers program that the endowment has sponsored since 1973, the Summer Seminars for Secondary School Teachers program nevertheless took its own direction from the outset. The unifying principle of the seminars is the close study of major texts in the humanities. The program was extremely successful in the first year; the fifteen pilot seminars, each with fifteen participants, drew over 2,400 applicants for 225 places. Thanks to the success of the pilot program and to the grant made to the endowment by the Andrew W. Mellon Foundation, the program sponsored fifty-one seminars in the summer of 1984 and sixty in 1985.

Structure

The seminars are held on the campuses of colleges and universities throughout the country. Under the direction of a distinguished teacher and scholar, usually a faculty member at the host institution, the seminars focus on texts from various periods in history, literature, philosophy, and religion. The major contours of the program remain the same in all seminars: the close reading of major texts in the humanities studied intensively and for their own sake. As a cooperative venture between secondary schools and institutions of higher learning, the seminars program provides for secondary school teachers what college teachers more readily take for granted, namely, a lively and contributing scholarly community.

Equally significant, the seminars give the participants opportunities that are needed but for the most part missing in their teaching careers. Opportunities for serious intellectual reflection can often be a casualty of the hectic and demanding schedules that secondary school teachers have to observe. Coaching, moderating, completing forms, guiding, and monitoring too often fill out a school day already crowded by the demanding standard teaching load. Deliberately, these seminars present a contrast, an opportunity to do one thing for an extended period of time: to read, think, and discuss without distractions. The seminars were designed so that the sessions would be intense—usually scheduled about four times a week for 2 or 2½ hours each time. The seminars in the pilot program, in fact, expanded the schedule; as discussions spilled out over into the lunch hour, new meeting times were hastily arranged to cover the material crowded out of the regular sessions. But even with all these demands, as well as the extraordinary social interconnections that developed in the course of a seminar, there were still large amounts of free time for thinking, for delving into the library, for rereading the text. The contrast here is not simply with the day-to-day and year-to-year realities of teaching but also with most other educational opportunities available to secondary school teachers. Teachers institutes, for example, valuable as they are, often make a point of filling up the day with lectures and discussions. One of the participants from a summer seminar on *War and Peace* declared that the most vital part of the seminar for her was the opportunity to read the novel three times in the course of a summer. Nothing else offered by the program could be simpler or more obvious. But the point is worth making that teachers can (and from their accounts, many do) go twenty years without having an opportunity to read at such a leisured pace. This program reminds us that all good teaching is rooted in knowledge and love of one's subject and that, if this knowledge and love are to flourish, the simplicity fostered by this program is not only a virtue but a necessity.

The opportunity for extended discussion presents the participants with the occasion to give the texts the attention great works deserve. When I visited the seminar on lyric poetry conducted by Helen Vendler, I observed a forceful example of close scrutiny of a text. The subject for the day was Keats, more specifically the "Ode to Melancholy." Vendler asked, "Who wants to begin?" One of the participants gave a careful, obviously well-considered, and thorough explication of the poem that lasted for about ten minutes. Classroom habits are apparently deeply ingrained in my mind. I waited for the group to move on to the next poem. Instead, Vendler simply said, "That's a good start," and the seminar took off from there. The excitement was almost palpable; sixteen interested readers spent the next hour probing more deeply into the poem, far more than I would have thought possible.

I like this example not only because Helen Vendler is such a good advertisement for the program and because the group of teachers itself was a model of energy and excitement but also because the two-stepped model that I witnessed—beginning where discussions more often end—is in some ways a paradigm for the experience of many participants. They came to these seminars from teaching situations in which a text or an idea must be swallowed in quick gulps. They were used to the problems of making texts and ideas immediately attractive to their audience of secondary school students. What they were not accustomed to was having extra time, more time, enough time. By their own admission, it took a while to get back into shape, to do the stretching and bending that allow one to spend, for example, ninety minutes on a fifteen-line poem. As soon as it became clear to them that they had left the fast-food franchise of the mind in favor of a six-week banquet, their next step was to see, in fact, how deeply into the material they could go. In my travels from seminar to seminar, I saw how immersed they all were in the subject matter. It is not as if they would discuss nothing but the topic of the seminar. We talked food, we talked baseball, we talked school politics, and we talked about the rewards and problems of secondary school education; but everything discussed was being reexamined in the light of their experience of intense study.

Results

The spirit of collegiality and the fostering of an academic community are explicit aims of this program. Such collegiality is necessary, of course, simply to accomplish the work of the seminar; that is, the effectiveness of the seminar depends on its members continually learning from one another. My observation was that they not only found good reason to respect one another but saw much to admire as well. They had one another as resource and example. On several occasions I heard some variation on this theme: "I'm working as hard as I am because I don't want to disappoint the others." And this mutual learning, as I have already suggested, spilled over into the many social situations engendered by the seminar. Many participants noted that the continuation of seminar business at the lunch table was the real proof that the seminars were working.

Other consequences of forming a genuine community of learning should also be mentioned. One of the most important discoveries the participants made was that they were not alone, that there were others like them who loved books and learning and ideas and who had thought long and hard about how to convey that love to their students. This is not to say that all participants characteristically thought of themselves as lone voices crying out in the wilderness of their own schools—although, to be honest, the motif of being a prophet without honor did occur from time to time in the discussions at which I was present. Rather, in the day-to-day activities of the school year, colleagues were, by necessity, less sources of intellectual stimulation for one another than busy coworkers who at best shared hurried coffeebreaks from time to time. Moreover, even when purely intellectual discussions occurred in a school setting, the participants usually had different academic interests and had read different books. Here all of a sudden were fifteen people united by the intensity of their interest in the same texts. That they would discover other common interests, especially with regard to their teaching, was inevitable. The cross-fertilization that ensued was aided by the wide variety of teaching conditions and geographical locations that the group represented: rural and urban, east and west, public and private. Their teaching experiences were equally varied and ranged from three years to thirty (we ask seminar directors, in selecting the participants, to give preference to applicants who have been teaching for at least three years). Together in one seminar to read Thucydides, Plutarch, and Bede were a teacher from a rural Alaskan village whose courses include both history and sled making, teachers from inner-city Chicago and Detroit, and a preparatory school classics teacher from Mississippi.

This cross-fertilization was also aided by the distinctive traditions, location, and resources of the school where the seminar was held. In the pilot program, we began a policy, which we hope will continue from year to year, of offering seminars at a variety of institutions. Harvard and Yale, Gonzaga in Spokane, and the State University of New York College at Geneseo were all sites for the first year. One reason for this diversity is of course obvious: the distinguished teaching that is expected from a seminar director is to be found in all types of institutions. Another reason comes into play as well. Clearly one of the important concerns of the program is to help break down some of the barriers between secondary schools and institutions of higher learning. The wrong signal goes out if only large research institutions are represented in the program. To include only such universities would reinforce a barrier that already exists by implying a caste system for the various kinds of colleges and universities in the country. The program cannot encourage what it does not itself exemplify. The participants were all delighted with the resources of their particular institutions, partly because all the directors did such a good job of fostering the sense of community that comes from being made welcome at a place, partly because the participants saw the place itself as an embodiment of their opportunity to do something significantly different from anything that they had done before. Resources at the various locations, however different they might be from each other, all functioned to remind the participants that they had a free forum to pursue the life of the mind.

Not surprisingly, the communities that formed during the summer live on in a number of ways. Seminar members have made a point of staying in touch. Several of the seminars have established newsletters; others are working on writing projects that developed from the work of the seminar. Participants in different seminars but from the same geographical region have met to exchange ideas and have helped advertise the program at regional conferences. Moreover, interaction during the seminars was not limited to the director and fifteen participants. Other faculty members at the seminar location had much to contribute and much to learn, through lectures, lunches, and informal conversations. In short, the kinds of networks that college and university teachers have traditionally been able to draw on are now beginning to develop for secondary school teachers as well.

Evaluation

Praise from participants, directors, and indeed anyone associated with the program has been high, to say the least. The program has been hailed in the media and has received write-ups in *Time* and the *New York Times*, among other places. Given the danger that such praise, even if justified, can easily turn into hype, I would like to end with an anecdote that sets a limit to what has been accomplished even as it highlights the goals of the program. Directors for the program are chosen in the same way that endowment grants are reviewed: panels of outside experts read the applications and recommend to the NEH chairman those that they believe will produce the best seminars. At the beginning of a panel meeting to choose the directors for 1984, Giles Constable, the eminent medieval historian and former director of Dumbarton Oaks—and a scholar who had done much to help publicize the program—looked up and said with almost no trace of irony, "Well, this is a good start. The endowment is to be congratulated. But tell me, when are you going to begin seminars for college teachers that are directed by secondary school teachers." Clearly, as I implied at the beginning of this essay, one of the goals of the program is to show that teachers at different levels ought to be seen as equally important members of the academic community who perform equally valuable services for society. Constable's suggestion takes this premise one logical step further by asserting in the strongest possible terms that teachers at all levels have much to give one another and much to learn from one another. But this truth is not universally acknowledged in the academic community. As it stands now, college teachers for the most part do not know how much they have to learn from secondary school teachers. (Exceptions, I would hasten to add, are the directors of the secondary school seminars.) Until the academic community feels comfortable with such a proposal, we still have a long way to go in breaking down the barriers between secondary schools and institutions of higher learning. But I think that this program and the promise of its long-term continuation are not a bad start.

Editor's Note

This essay and the following one should be read together since the first outlines a major school-college collaborative program sponsored by the National Endowment for the Humanities, and the second offers a specific example of the program in operation.

Gonzaga University: National Endowment for the Humanities Summer Seminar: The Quest for Love and Knowledge

Franz Schneider

From 26 June to 5 August 1984, fifteen men and women met at Gonzaga University in Spokane, Washington, to pioneer one of the newly inaugurated National Endowment for the Humanities (NEH) Summer Seminars for Secondary School Teachers. Our chosen topic was The Quest for Love and Knowledge in Dante's *Divine Comedy* and Goethe's *Faust*. When we began, none of the participants could have imagined how soon and how intensely the Dantean and Faustian quests would turn into our own.

Format

In view of the subject matter, it was inevitable that the seminar would turn into an intense experience for the participants, for few things are more central in our lives than the search for meaning and the striving for values that give purpose to our existence. And in this process love and knowledge play the decisive motivating role. It was precisely for this reason that we selected the great poems of Dante and Goethe. As emblems of human striving, furthermore, love and knowledge could hardly have been treated separately. They serve to define each other and express each other, because for Dante and Goethe—as for many others in this ancient and venerable tradition—love cannot exist without knowledge, and vice versa. Both are necessary for union, whether human or divine.

Consequently, the seminar not only dealt with the quest for love and knowledge in general but also looked specifically at some of the digressive journeys prompted by the quest and at the ways they colored the various types of love (courtly, stil-nuovist, romantic, mystic) and the different modes of knowledge (natural-revealed, scientific-religious, white-magic–black-magic) in the two poems. The influence of these themes on contemporary culture provided another powerful stimulus for seminar discussion.

It is clear from this description that the seminar was neither a teacher's institute dealing with methods and curricula nor a graduate seminar devoted to the fine points of scholarship or to a professional discipline like literary criticism or theory. The seminar simply gave its fifteen members an opportunity to read carefully and leisurely two important literary works and then to discuss this experience in a "grand conversation" that would explore the shape and nature of these works and likewise test the validity and implications they have for people living in the present.

For this reason, we endeavored to have as many subject areas represented in the seminar as was possible. A committee of four—a college English professor, a high school English teacher, a former middle school principal who also served as assistant director, and the director—chose the participants, with great difficulty, after carefully scrutinizing seventy-five excellent applications that had survived the initial screening process. Special attention was given to the applicants' personal statements, and the final determination was inevitably influenced by evidence of creativity, versatility, extraordinary dedication to students, and the promise of successful participation in an experimental intellectual venture.

The group of teachers in art, history, literature, and language that emerged from the selection process—we never found the mathematician or scientist we had hoped for—did not disappoint. They had no problem in keeping the seminar focused on the text, on reading, and on discussion. In fact, the discussions were so lively that we always ran out of time. There was such a richness of character, expertise, and talent of all kinds represented that for long stretches we actually experienced that most elusive of all utopias: a community of learners—one heart, one mind, one soul.

At least, this unity is reflected in the journals that all participants were required to keep. To give some structure to the discussions and reflection, we also asked each participant for two reports. One of these assignments was to paraphrase part of the text, to prepare a synopsis of a scene or an event, or to summarize cantos or acts so that major issues or conflicts could be dramatized. The second report had to do with working out moral, allegorical, and anagogical meanings of the text. The participants could either take a subjective and personal approach or offer analyses based on material from secondary sources. At most meetings, teams of two gave their reports at the beginning of a given session to initiate discussion.

The seminar structure, in other words, was kept deliberately simple. We met three times a week from nine to noon on Monday, Wednesday, and Friday (or Thursday, as the occasion dictated). During the mornings—and sometimes afternoons—of Tuesday and Thursday, the director also met with the scheduled reporting teams to explore the themes, approaches, and problems that seemed most in keeping with the issues raised by the syllabus. Of course, the syllabus was merely a guide. The participants themselves made the final choices about the materials to be presented. As a result we had reports that ranged from rigorous scholarly analyses to quasi-dramatic presentations complete with music and artistic illustrations.

In addition, an occasional seminar or afternoon period was used for a straight lecture by a visiting scholar, or for a colloquium led by the director. Such occasions were dubbed "everything-you-ever-wanted-to-know-about . . . sessions." The topics covered provided background, dealing with difficult ideas and stimulating thought about their current relevance. For example, in studying Dante we dealt with the *dolce stil nuovo* and the politics of the *De monarchia*, Aristotle and Boethius, Thomas Aquinas, and Siger of Brabant. For Goethe, we followed the ramifications of the Faust myth in American literature and in the stunning film *Mephisto*, a fascinating chronicle of theater, politics, and power in Nazi Germany.

Other films we saw included Cocteau's treatments of the Tristan and Orpheus myths, interesting to us not only for the complex of passionate love but also for the infernal descents on either a literal or a symbolic level. But watching these films proved more than an intellectual exercise. Fortuitously, the discussions afterward turned into such convivial socials that the group lost no time in arranging a full schedule of picnics, luncheons, dinners, and parties of all kinds. Expressions of collegiality of this sort are exceedingly important. Their success or failure can make or break a seminar.

Another advantage the seminar had was the environment: Gonzaga University, the city of Spokane, and the surrounding region. Two universities and two colleges, as well as several big hospitals, make Spokane the largest educational and medical center between Minneapolis and Seattle. From there the visitor has easy access to some of the most beautiful regions of the United States and Canada. As one would expect, seminar participants took full advantage of this geographical paradise.

Founded by the Jesuits and still administered by them, Gonzaga is a small university with a normal enrollment of thirty-five hundred students during the academic year but a much smaller contingent in the summer. In this friendly, congenial place red tape is kept at a minimum and the liberal arts are still part of each student's general curriculum. In keeping with this tradition, the administration and staff did everything in their power to make us feel welcome. In fact, the academic vice-president gave a reception for us and treated us to a formal dinner that we all fondly remember as Beatrice's Beatific Banquet; or, the Conveniat of Convivial Consort.

The Experience

It is difficult to describe the seminar experience accurately or to provide an adequate summary of all we learned. Great works of literature, like great mountain massifs, demand a multitude of partial ascents and descents before the journey can end in the final climb and return. And in some works, these movements up and down become the literal shape of the story, as they do in *The Divine Comedy* and, to some extent, *Faust*. Dante and Faust must brave the depth and achieve the mountain—be it Purgatory, Brocken, or the High Mountains of act 4, part 2—before they can even hope to catch a view of the true condition of reality or sense an intimation of that unity and harmony of "being" which they so fervently desire.

The routes we took up the slopes to the summits of the *Comedy* and *Faust* were charted by the theme of love and knowledge. They involved not an incidental hike or an excursionary walk but a laborious effort up a steep trail, gradually becoming a bona fide climb to the top. For both Dante and Goethe believed that it was the quality of a person's love and knowledge—two tracks of the same path—that would either damn or save. Everything these authors wrote is ultimately reduced to the kind of love and knowledge that invites moral mimesis and that determines the ultimate fate of souls. In the *Artist's Journey into the Interior* Erich Heller defines the terms of this fate when he comments on Faust's damnation:

> [W]hat else is salvation if not the fulfillment of a destiny in the integrity of Being, what else damnation if not the agony of the creature without destiny forever unreachable, in monstrous singularity, by any intimations of a surpassingly sensible

coherence, and forever debarred, in his short, uncertain, anxious, and perishable
life, from any contact with something lasting, sure, serene, and incorruptible?   (20)

For Dante, integrity of being is an attribute of God. One can come into vital
contact with it by loving him and his creation through a proper exercise of faith
and reason, which predisposes one to recognize and obey the revealed will of
the creator. Truth is what befits human beings to know and love, what they
are meant to know and love. But reason and love go astray: the former by mere
curiosity unrestrained by wisdom, the latter by excess or deficiency of desire,
or by choice of the wrong object.

For Goethe the matter is more complicated. He, too, cannot divorce the problem of knowledge from the totality of human nature, or the aspirations of the
mind from the destiny of the soul. But he cannot show with as much certitude
as Dante can what this destiny and totality are made of. Consequently, as Heller
points out, we have in Goethe two overpowering and paradoxical intuitions:
"that man's *being* was definable only through his incessant striving to *become*
what he was not yet and what was *yet* meant to be; and that in this striving
he was in extreme danger of losing himself through his impatient and impetu-
ous ignorance of what he was" (31). Hence we find in Faust a man who out
of despair of knowledge—even the knowledge of black magic that unlocks the
secrets of the universe—turns to love so that he can maintain his impetus.

There is one thing the two authors seem to have in common in spite of their
different theological beliefs and the differences inherent in their respective ages
and cultures: the realization that human beings are capable of evil and free to
embrace it, especially by committing "sins of the mind" (Heller 30). How we
argued about the sins of the mind and how we failed to come to a consensus
on this matter! Yet we did agree that searching out "truths" destructive to human nature and the nature of the universe and doing things in excess of a person's being came pretty close to a definition we could work with. Like Dante
and Goethe we were troubled by the ability of the mind to rise above the reality
of being and coldly and objectively destroy this reality. Like them, we could
envision only one antidote to the poison of cold, nihilistic intellectuality: love.

As a poet of love, Dante seemed the more complex and profound of the
two. His protagonist's love for Beatrice is not only the worship of the *dolce stil
nuovo* poet for his lady as symbol and inspiration of intellectual beauty but
also the ambiguous courtly love of the troubadour whose origins may be rooted
in a dark and destructive eros. Both these loves undergo catharsis and purga-
tion. They are converted into the love of the mystic for a saintly person who,
as a *figura* of revelation and grace, mediates between the mystic and God. This
transformation is made still more complicated by Dante's refusal to let go of the
world of sense and dense historical reality when he constructs his metaphoric
prefigurations of eternal truth.

There is some element of courtly love in the Faust-Gretchen relationship
also. But Gretchen is never far from serving as yet another instrument in Faust's
quest for knowledge: his search for the innermost parts of life and matter as
well as the outermost parts of heaven and earth. For Faust, Gretchen is not an
expression of "the light of faith," as Beatrice is for Dante, but an expression of,
as the pansophists would have said, "the light of nature." Yet, whereas the pansophists had wanted to penetrate through the cosmos to God in an objective

fashion, Faust's quest is portrayed as the human ego's striving to be as large as the world and, perhaps, as God himself.

Consequently, Faust's love for Gretchen, though rooted in the libido restored to him by Mephistopheles, is still another way of expanding his ego after suffering the crushing defeats of a middle-aged Titan of scholarship condemned to the fruitless pursuit of licit and illicit knowledge. This knowledge would have destroyed him had not the Eternal Feminine, in a gratuitous act of grace, sent her messengers to snatch him away from the lascivious Mephisto and his minions.

Syllabus

Although there was nothing ironclad about the syllabus, we never strayed far from the thematic boundaries it suggested. What Goethe considers a law of life— "in der Beschränkung liegt das Geheimnis"—holds true also here: the secret of freedom comes by way of limitation. Free discussion becomes fruitful only if there is something to discuss. Seminar directors must never forget that the participants are teachers who have just finished a gruelling year when they arrive and who will be going back to heavy workloads soon after the seminar is over.

Theme: The Quest for Love and Knowledge in *The Divine Comedy* and *Faust*

Monday, June 27: Introduction
    Information and procedures
    The text and bibliography
    The epic journey: the way up is the way down; through error to salvation
    The myth of the descent and mid-life crisis
    Homeric and Vergilian precedents
Wednesday, June 29: *Inferno* (Canto 1): The Dark Wood of Error
    The allegory of the three beasts and the heavenly (not magic) mountain
    Divine love and evil
    The allegory of love
Friday, July 1: *Inferno* (Canto 5): The Passionate Lovers
    The story of Paolo and Francesca; Dante's fainting
    Dante's love for Beatrice
    Courtly love
    Tschaikowsky: "Francesca da Rimini, Symphonic Fantasy after Dante"
Wednesday, July 6: *Inferno* (Canto 26): The Evil Counselors
    The story of Ulysses
    Knowledge, heresy, and Dante's unorthodox quest
    The Ulysses theme: Homer, Vergil, Tennyson
Friday, July 8: *Purgatorio* (Cantos 16–18): The Central Cantos
    The doctrine of free will, conscience, and love
    The problem of the doctrine that "all is love" and the fact of punishment and damnation for love
    Dante's lethargy and sloth
Monday, July 11: *Purgatorio* (Canto 1, Cantos 7–9)
    Cato, the serpent, and the dream of the eagle
    The limitation of human reason (the unconscious and the mystery of evil)
    The figural imagination

Wednesday, July 13: *Purgatorio* (Cantos 27–33): The Earthly Paradise
    Vergil and Beatrice
    Love and knowledge and human senses
    The symbolic and angelic imagination
Friday, July 15: *Paradiso* (Cantos 23, 28–33): Mirrors of Light
    The "transhumanizing" of Dante
    The problem of human sight confronted by the essence of godhead
    Metaphors of music, color, motion, geometric forms, and light as representations
        of divine reality
Monday, July 18: *Paradiso* (Cantos 31, 33): The Mystical Rose and "The Triune Circle
        of One Magnitude"
    Dante's vision of heaven and of God
    Beatrice's disappearance
    The human image "within" the image of God
Wednesday, July 20: Summary, Retrospect, Prospect
    The poet of heaven and the poet of earth
    "The light of heaven" (revealed knowledge) and the "light of nature" (natural
        knowledge)
    Goethe's Christian symbolism and secular purpose
Friday, July 22: The Scholar's Tragedy: Faust's Monologues
    "Night Scene" (354–480; 602–732; 762–84)
    "Outside the City Gates" (903–40; 1064–99)
    "Study" (1178–258)
    Knowledge, suicide, and black magic
    Mephisto's wager with the Lord and Faust
Monday, July 25: The Scholar's Tragedy and Monologues continued
    "Evening" (2687–728)
    "Forest and Cave" (3117–250; 3431–58)
    "A Field" (both prose and monologues)
    Temptation and compact
Wednesday, July 27: The Gretchen Tragedy: Monologue and Songs
    "Evening" (2759–804)
    "Gretchen's Chamber" (3374–413)
    "By the City Wall" (3587–617)
    "Cathedral Scene"
    "Dungeon" (4412–20)
    Private morality and public morality
    Gretchen's "kleine Welt"
Friday, July 29: *Faust, Part 2*: Synopsis and Act 1
    "Charming Landscape" (4679–727)
    "A Dark Gallery" (descent to the mothers)
    The problem of unifying Christian and pagan, classical and Romantic, gothic and
        Hellenic, German and Greek civilization
    Faust's "grosse Welt" and the "world" as parable, metaphor, symbol, and "Gleichnis"
Monday, August 1: *Faust, Part 2*: Act 5
    "Open Country: Philemon and Baucis"
    "Palace: The Three Mighty Men"
    "Deep Night: The Watchman's Song" (11288–2336) and Faust's exchange with
        Mephisto
    "Midnight: The Four Crones; Faust and Care"
    Ideal ends and sordid means
    Faust's ambiguous death and salvation
Wednesday, August 3: Beginning, Middle, and End

Dukas, *The Sorcerer's Apprentice*
Mussorgsky, *On Bald Mountain*
"Mountain Gorges; Forest Cliffs; Wilderness" (11844–2111)
Mahler's *Choral Symphony*, no. 8
The problem of the momentary selfish enjoyment of sexual desire and the enduring
    creative urgency stimulated by the imaginative spiritualization of love
Replacement of the Lord of the prologue with the all-inclusive moving spirit of love
    at the end
Friday, August 5:
Dante or Goethe?
The meaning of *The Divine Comedy* and *Faust* for today
Celebration

Evaluation

As with all pilot programs, two questions must be asked: Was the seminar worth
the cost and effort? Was it successful? The answer to both in this case must be
a resounding yes—at least from the standpoint of the participants and the director. Of course, the emphasis put on the various aspects of the experience differed
from one person to the next. But all commented favorably, if not with outright
and unabashed enthusiasm, on the great power of renewal they felt as a result
of the intellectual exchange with their fellow teachers and the affirming friend-
ships created by this process.

Such professional and personal enrichment also benefited the host institution. As a university in which every student is required to take a solid general
course in liberal studies with a heavy component in the humanities, Gonzaga
often feels pressure to offer more vocational and preprofessional training. Events
like the summer seminar counteract this pressure and promote greater understanding within the university and the civic community of what the humanities
are all about. Reports on television and radio and in the local press brought
significant accolades for the university and the NEH. Residents of the area saw
the seminar as evidence that we are serious about the new drive for academic
excellence in American education, alumni were impressed, and some colleagues
in the meantime have submitted proposals for seminars of their own (one of
which was funded for the summer of 1985).

There were, to be sure, the usual glitches, irritants, and problems that cu-
mulatively could have spelled disaster. For instance, a week before the start of
the seminar there was a fire in the dormitory where we had reserved space for
women's housing. The good and speedy work of our assistant director solved
that problem by finding even better quarters in a smaller and newer building.
Unfortunately, their distance from the men's dormitory and the housing for the
handicapped (one of our group needed access by wheelchair) occasionally in-
terfered with the unified operation we planned.

Another low point came when the rain washed out our boat cruise on Lake
Coeur d'Alene and up the St. Joe's River. However, dinners like "Vergil's Vigil"
at the Spaghetti Factory, Schneider's little Sommerfest, and picnics like the one
in the Priest Lake Wilderness in Northern Idaho made up for the disappointment. One of our best experiences was the open house to which our Idaho member had invited us. He had built his own home on a hilltop in a private bird

sanctuary above Lake Coeur d'Alene. In this beautiful spot we spent an after-noon and early evening sharing poetry, drama, music, and art—others' and our own. It was here that we first felt that special sense of community that we celebrated in our farewell banquet, the Ring of the White Rose.

The most serious problem we encountered had to do with how the seminar itself was conceived. Dante and Goethe are an overwhelming combination for a mere six weeks. We would have done better to confine ourselves to either the *Comedy* or *Faust*. As it was, too much material had to be summarized, and not enough attention was paid to structural and linguistic matters. Because our li-brary is somewhat limited, we should have made more use of the interlibrary loan system to obtain important commentaries that could not be obtained locally.

The translations of the text and their apparatus also proved more than a passing vexation. Although we had chosen the Ciardi translation as the com-mon vehicle, many members would have preferred other texts, such as those by Bickersteth, Bergin, Binyon, Carlyle, Cary, Huse, Longfellow, Sayers, and Sinclair. (None had yet seen Allen Mandelbaum's fine translation or read George P. Elliott's essay "Getting to Dante," *Hudson Review*, 11.4 [1958–59]: 597–609, which is still one of the best short treatments of this problem.)

As for the *Faust* translation, participants found Walter Arndt's work and the section on criticism in the Norton edition acceptable. What did displease now and again was the occasional preciousness and abstruseness of the editor's (Cyrus Hamlin's) interpretive notes. On the other hand, both Arndt and Ham-lin did succeed in conveying to English-speaking readers the beauty and strength of Goethe's poetry, convincing them that Goethe is a great poet—no small achievement.

On balance, the seminar was a great success. The opinion was unanimous that the summer program for secondary teachers is one of the best things that the NEH has done for the humanities in America. Indeed, many participants stayed in touch with one another and exchanged course plans and class materials that they had worked out in the summer of 1984. Some have even taught one another's classes. There is a lot of evidence that what one of the participants said in her evaluation is true: "We did, indeed, often feel like a large and happy family." So the wish expressed again and again in correspondence and conver-sation is not too surprising: "Let's have 'Dante or Goethe Revisited' a few year's hence." Until then, we proudly wear splendid T-shirts, designed by one of our artists, that depict Goethe and Dante against a mountain and a river of the Pa-cific Northwest—Goethe gazing straight ahead into the future and Dante's se-vere profile scrutinizing him skeptically while looking at the world askance.

Utah State University: Northern Utah's English Articulation Program

Joyce Kinkead, William Smith, and Pat Stoddart

In February 1982, David Pierpont Gardner, president of the University of Utah and chair of the National Commission on Excellence in Education, announced new admissions requirements for students entering the University of Utah in 1986. As most of us read his newspaper article, "An Open Letter to High School Students and Their Parents," we marveled at the boldness of his announcement. As expected, the board of regents immediately required all four-year institutions within the state to follow Gardner's example and publicize their admissions requirements. Not only had Gardner drawn the line at accepting poorly prepared entering freshmen at the University of Utah, but he had also forced state public institutions into revising their admissions policies and rethinking their definitions of quality. His letter and the board of regents' directive implicitly demanded some degree of articulation among all the institutions of higher education in Utah. The state's approach to articulation, however, followed a top-down model of administration, focusing primarily on admissions policies and ignoring the needs and advice of the state's high schools. Most institutions in Utah responded to the board's demand as an exercise in crisis management and unilaterally publicized newly strengthened admissions requirements within three months. For most colleges articulation ended at the admissions office, where prospective students and their parents could apply for information about the requirements. In retrospect, Gardner's proclamation, originally viewed as arrogant, was in fact a timely and needed educational strategy that shook the entire state out of its complacency and forced it to address important educational issues.

Utah State University's Role in the Articulation Model

The administration and faculty of Utah State University immediately rejected the state's implicit definition of articulation on philosophical grounds: Gardner's model conflicted with the mission of the land-grant institution by denying admission to rural students whose high schools could not provide the educational requirements demanded by the University of Utah. In essence, Gardner would restrict his campus to students "with the skill and ability to cope with the courses they would be required to take" during their college careers. And since Utah has no two-year-college system, many students disqualified by the new model would have no public institution within the state in which to develop the mandated skills. Gardner apparently assumed that the elementary and high schools would somehow mysteriously align their curricula to meet his institution's new requirements. Instead of revising its admission requirements in vacuo, Utah State University sought help from the local school districts that supplied a large number of its freshmen, focusing on two that contributed approximately 625 students to an average freshman class enrollment of 1,500. Enlisting the aid of high school students, college students who had graduated from its larger "feeder" schools, parents, and classroom teachers and administrators from elementary schools and secondary schools, Utah State University initiated an articulation committee that developed its own model.

The English Articulation Committee

The committee laid the groundwork for the Utah State model at its first meeting. The participants divided quite naturally into four groups—an articulation steering committee, a counseling and study-skills committee, a mathematics committee, and an English committee—and began meeting regularly during the summer of 1982, with all members serving voluntarily. One of the most active committees was the ten-member English Articulation Committee, consisting of three high school English teachers, two college English teachers, an English education teacher, a principal, a parent, and curriculum coordinators from a city school and from the state office of education. In Utah, as in many other states, colleges and universities had waged war against the admission of ill-prepared students for more than a decade, allocating thousands of dollars to "remedial" programs. Now the English Articulation Committee saw as one of its major goals the development of a more comprehensive method of preparing basic writers for college than Utah State was capable of carrying out alone.

At the first meeting we learned how insulated we all were. Few of us seemed to know what the others were doing. In fact, Utah State's English department had been quite cavalier about publishing its requirements as soon as it had changed them. We had gone our own way without realizing the impact our curricular changes had on our feeder high schools. We had assumed, as Gene Maeroff points out in his article "Ties That Do Not Bind," that "college freshmen are born into this world with no previous schooling," an attitude we seldom acknowledged until a poorly prepared student entered our classrooms and forced us to exclaim, "What are they learning in the high schools?" On the other hand, the local high schools had not realized that we did not require a research paper in freshman English, that we had initiated a placement essay, that students had several ways of waiving writing courses, that a writing center existed, and that our writing program had changed from a competency-based program to a student-centered program. At the conclusion of our first articulation meeting, one thing was abundantly clear: we needed to communicate with one another.

During the summer the English Articulation Committee planned a method of aligning high school and college curricula. All of us were tired of the ways we had been doing things. For years, whenever we assigned a term paper, English teachers in local high schools assigned term papers to their college-bound juniors and seniors. If we taught *Crime and Punishment,* then sixteen-year-olds all over northern Utah read *Crime and Punishment.* Because of this curricular mirroring the students in our introduction-to-literature classes were constantly complaining, "I read this in high school."

By the summer's end, we knew that a well-designed high school curriculum should prepare students for college, not simply replicate a college curriculum. We also learned that we at the college level had been remiss in not informing our future teachers that the methods we used to teach Camus to twenty-year-olds were not the same methods we would use to teach Paul Zindel to fifteen-year-olds. We had ignored the middle and junior high school levels in preparing teachers, not realizing the differences that distinguish their student bodies from older groups. With the exception of an adolescent-literature course, the department offered no methods course in the teaching of literature. At the suggestion of middle school English teachers, our English department planned two new undergraduate courses emphasizing the teaching of literature and the teaching of reading in the high schools. The two new courses, Literature for Teachers and Reading for Teachers, supplemented our existing courses in writing methods. Again, it was apparent that, while all of us were making assumptions, few of us were ever testing those assumptions or, worse yet, discussing them with the people they most seriously affected.

But perhaps the single most important communication to arise from the summer meetings between the high school English departments and the Utah State English department is a one-page document outlining the "general background in English" that Utah State would like entering students to possess. What we agreed on were not specific writing assignments—the 500-word theme, the five-paragraph essay, the literary research paper—but the writing skills and experiences students should have before entering the university's English program. For example, we all believe that high school graduates should be able to write sustained prose with only minimal errors in spelling, punctuation, and grammar. Moreover, we all believe that they should have written in different modes for different audiences and had their work exposed to peer criticism as an important part of the writing process. Within three months our articulation program had become one of sharing and informing, not of telling one another what to do. By listening to one another carefully without preconceptions about what to expect, we had inductively developed an "open-communications articulation model."

We began the next series of meetings by simply showing high school English teachers what college teachers do in class. In November 1982 the Department of English conducted a half-day workshop demonstrating how Utah State English teachers grade papers and why. The college teachers fought the temptation to tell the high school teachers how to conduct secondary classes; instead, they focused on what they themselves do best—teach college students. At other meetings, high school teachers reciprocated our evaluation workshops by sharing their papers and their methods of evaluation with us. During informal discussions after these sessions, we usually discovered areas of agreement and places where we could align our curricula.

The Role of the Writing Center in Articulation

As the committee recommended closer cooperation with local high schools, it became evident that the English department had to provide a central place where secondary and college teachers could coordinate their efforts and communicate openly. The departmentally operated Writing Center seemed ideal for this purpose because it was already established on campus as a place for faculty colloquiums, intradepartmental grading sessions, and in-service programs. Since the Writing Center had been organized to accommodate various audiences, the committee felt that one more would not harm its effectiveness. The on-campus articulation that the center fostered among departments also made it an appropriate site for extending the university's boundaries beyond the campus.

In the fall of 1983, after one year's planning, the Writing Center implemented several of the articulation committee's recommendations: strengthening the placement essay, publishing samples of "effective" student writing, creating new methods courses, and implementing a series of high school writing workshops. Since the administrative structure for the existing placement essay was foundering, the English department revamped it as the first step toward an articulation program and as a symbol of its good faith in carrying out the suggestions of the committee. The placement essay provides a tangible point of articulation between high school and college English programs. Students, parents, and teachers usually receive information about the placement test during summer orientation. The test involves writing two essays, which are graded holistically by full-time faculty members from disciplines across campus. Since a university-wide faculty discuss and evaluate the papers, the idea of quality in writing permeates the campus and filters its way into the high schools as a requirement for future history, engineering, and language majors as well as future English majors. We now plan to invite high school teachers from all disciplines to participate in scoring the placement essays. As high school and college faculty members discuss the quality of the essays, new ground for further articulation will be broken.

The Writing Center staff complied in an innovative way with the articulation committee's suggestion about publishing student writing. In 1983 the Writing Center and the English department published an anthology of writing from the freshman class. This collection provides model essays for students to study and discuss as they undertake the same assignments; in addition, it shows students that their work is "publishable" as James Moffett recommends. Moreover, the English department converts royalties from the book into cash prizes for the best student writing of the academic year. The anthology not only serves an important pedagogical function on campus but also provides high school teachers and students with samples of what the Utah State faculty considers good writing. And symbolically the anthology tells our future students that we value clear thinking and effective writing.

Although the Writing Center cannot offer courses as the English department does, it has immeasurably helped the articulation program by providing a supervised teaching practicum for undergraduate teaching majors. Students enrolled in Diagnosing Writing Problems experience firsthand the difficulties basic writers have with the written language. Students tutor beginning writers on a one-to-one basis in the Writing Center, translating classroom lectures into practical approaches. The advantages of this participation are many: students mature intellectually, socially, and emotionally, ultimately becoming better student teachers when they serve apprenticeships with our secondary colleagues.

Besides sharing consultants who come to campus for workshops and conventions, the Writing Center offers summer workshops with outside consultants who direct their material specifically toward public school teachers. More important, the Writing Center frequently provides the only meeting ground for university faculty members and high school students by offering a series of small-group writing workshops. During the academic year high school students visit the Writing Center, bringing with them drafts of papers they are working on in their classes. Full-time members of the English faculty evaluate the papers, asking the students questions that lead to significant revisions. From the contacts made in the Writing Center between future freshmen and university faculty members numerous benefits have accrued: the department views high school writing firsthand, the undergraduate tutors observe faculty members in action, and the department gets one more chance to recruit students. Another, more practical benefit is the professional relationship that develops between high school and university teachers through a series of classroom exchanges. Composition students at the high schools and the university write letters to each other, one group asking questions about writing, the other group responding. In yet another exchange, English education majors take a course in which they critically review essays written by high school students.

There are both advantages and disadvantages to relying on the Writing Center as the focal point of the articulation program. For one thing, the effort required to keep the articulation going sometimes overextends the center's resources and staff through meetings, administrative planning, and visits to high school campuses. Although the work is rewarding, the constant demands are enervating. Even so, the successes of the articulation program far outweigh the temporary problems that increased funding could solve. An awareness of writing standards and a discernible change in attitudes toward writing are now apparent among both students and faculty members within the department, across our campus, and in the high schools of northern Utah.

Logan High School's Role in Articulation

At the high school level, important changes took place as the cooperative spirit of the committee and of the Writing Center increased. The leading example of how articulation should function within our open-communications model of articulation is Logan High School, the largest of five participating feeder schools and the source of nearly twenty-five percent of Utah State's entering freshman class. Early in the articulation committee's deliberations it became obvious that, although both university and high school teachers agreed that good writing skills are necessary for college-bound students, neither knew what the other thought was good. After the initial in-service writing workshop in November 1982, the workshop was used for practical classroom purposes. On various occasions, classes of high school students have taken the first drafts of their papers to the Utah State University Writing Center. Professors and graduate students have read them, providing constructive criticism, supplementary guide sheets, and supportive materials for the students to use in rewriting their work. One opening line of a student's paper changed from "When I was quite young, my parents owned a small candy store. Later they gave it up" to "My parents sold their small candy store when I was five." Another sentence, "The police had the party surrounded," became "Blue uniforms nearly outnumbered T-shirts and jeans."

The articulation committee plans more of these exchanges because they transfer valuable college writing experiences not only to the high schools but also to their English curriculum directors.

It is a rarity when practical experiences occur on the bottom of the pyramid as a result of the philosophical meetings at the top. For years secondary teachers in northern Utah have felt the need to exchange ideas with one another and with university educators, but little was done until the Northern Utah Articulation Committee evolved at the urging of Utah State University. As a result of the articulation committee, a newly formed organization, the Council of Northern Utah English Teachers, composed of English department heads, meets monthly to organize informational workshops on such topics as assignment making and brain research and its implications for writing. We discuss the objectives of changes in curriculum and compare the advantages and disadvantages of changes in curricular practices in the various schools. Because these efforts have been rewarding, the future should offer more exchanges and more experimentation. Local schools, in particular Logan High School, will explore methods of attracting parents onto the committee. Parents should be made more aware of the successes of the articulation program and learn how to bring their desires to the committee's attention for incorporation into the curriculum. Parents must be invited to attend the in-service sessions and to visit the Writing Center to see the kinds of cooperation necessary for continuing a successful articulation program. Now with an open-communications model, the teachers and parents are better able to help seniors make the transition from high school to university.

Through a great deal of hard work, early morning summer meetings, and later afternoon winter meetings, we have developed a voluntary English articulation program. We now have a mechanism through which parents and high school teachers and administrators can have a major impact on our standards and curriculum. We have shared our fears with one another openly, airing our grievances publicly.

Our experience has taught us how to build a successful open-communications model, but there are caveats. Schools contemplating such a program should follow four steps. First, teachers and administrators from elementary school to college should be actively involved in all phases of the program. Second, articulation should occur in specific academic disciplines as well as in the traditional area of admissions. Third, parents and former high school students should be encouraged to participate in the program. And finally, a formal administrative structure must be created for the synthesis of ideas and the coordination of committee activity.

Granted, such an English articulation program does have its limitations. Participants in a voluntary program sometimes lose interest. And when the members of the committee have neither grants nor local funds to sustain them, they sometimes find that they have more pressing obligations than attending regularly scheduled meetings. Perhaps, our open-communications model will need legislation similar to that of the California model. Or perhaps, like the educators in Florida, we will find that a voluntary program ultimately needs structure and legislative intervention to "keep the cooperative spirit alive."

Illinois State University: The Cooperative Teaching Program

Ron Fortune and Janice Neuleib

Illinois State University's English department has a long history of articulation with high schools and community colleges in Illinois. Its faculty members have regularly been called on to conduct in-service workshops on teaching writing and on teaching literature and to evaluate the schools' self-study programs. That the department's highest degree is a Doctor of Arts epitomizes its commitment to English education at the secondary and postsecondary levels, for this degree specifically focuses on the application of literary and writing theory to the teaching of English at all grade levels.

Early Efforts

The department has gone beyond workshops and instructional programs, however, to distinguish itself in the area of school-college cooperation. Its faculty have directed or participated in a number of special statewide programs that either have had or promise to have a significant impact on the way English is taught in high schools and colleges throughout Illinois. For twenty-one years, the English department has hosted an annual conference for the heads of Illinois secondary English departments (HISED). Attracting over two hundred English department heads each year from high schools throughout Illinois, this conference gives those attending the chance to share ideas about how English instruction can be improved in their individual schools and about how they can address their administrative problems more effectively.

The department was also instrumental in initiating the Illinois English Articulation Project, which it now codirects at the request of the state board of higher education. This project explores ways to implement the recommendations of a task force on writing that the board commissioned four years ago to suggest ways of improving writing instruction in elementary, secondary, and postsecondary schools throughout the state. One of the project's first actions was to establish an articulation network for gathering and disseminating information on English programs at public schools and universities throughout the state. Through this information, the institutions can compare their programs with those of other schools around the state and perhaps discover new approaches that can help them improve their handling of common problems.

The English department's school-college cooperative efforts have been so substantial that the Fall 1983 issue of the *Illinois English Bulletin*, the official journal of the Illinois Association of Teachers of English, was dedicated to describing the most prominent of these achievements.

While the programs described above have done much to help the university's English department improve school-college cooperation throughout the state, our work with the schools has begun to move, within the last five years, in a new and what is proving to be a most rewarding direction. In addition to the programs conducted outside the classroom, we have begun to develop cooperative programs based on in-class work. Specifically, we are instituting programs that get English teachers into writing or literature classes at grade levels other than their own. We believe that the knowledge they acquire through their firsthand exposure to English teaching at a variety of grade levels will enable them to understand more thoroughly than they generally do the instructional problems that teachers at other levels must solve. And it is only when they understand these problems in detail that they can genuinely help these teachers devise appropriate solutions.

Background

Our focus on in-class work began in the spring of 1979 when the English departments at Illinois State and at Illinois Central, a community college in East Peoria, agreed to a teacher exchange in which one faculty member from the English department at ICC taught two freshman writing courses and a freshman literature course at ISU and a faculty member from the university's English department taught comparable courses at ICC. The cooperative arrangement here was limited to a university and a community college, but this articulation strategy in many ways determined the direction of future articulation efforts between ISU's English department and local elementary and secondary schools.

Although the teachers involved in this first experimental exchange had taught comparable courses at their home schools before beginning the project, they undertook the new assignments because they recognized that teaching at a university was not necessarily a good index to teaching at a community college and vice versa. The university teacher had regularly taught a graduate course concerned with English instruction in a two-year college. Through his participation in this exchange, he wanted to learn more about the types of courses that were the subject matter of his graduate course. The faculty member at the community college hoped to develop a better sense of how English courses at his community college correlated with university courses. The point here is that, despite their different motives for participating in the project, both instructors implicitly recognized that they could best understand the courses at the other school by teaching those courses and acquiring a firsthand knowledge of the classroom circumstances that dictated what the courses could and could not attempt.

In addition to teaching courses as visiting professors, both participants served on writing and curriculum committees in their host departments. These extracurricular assignments gave them a more thorough understanding of their courses, and they could see how these courses were shaped by the overall curricular plans of their temporary departments.

English department faculty members at Illinois State have extended the principles underlying the community college–university project to their interaction with writing teachers in a local high school. They have arranged for a member of their own writing faculty to teach a section of the university's freshman composition course at the high school each spring. This program resembles others around the country that give select groups of high school students the opportunity to earn college credit that they can claim when they begin college. However, because the course is part of an ongoing school-college cooperative program that stresses the direct exposure of teachers at one educational level to the educational circumstances at another, the university faculty member does not approach the experience in the same way that she would if she were simply giving a college writing course at a high school or teaching high school students in a class on campus.

Like the university teacher who took on a community college course, she has become as much a part of the high school faculty as her schedule allows. She meets with English department faculty members at the high school during her free time to discuss her experiences in the classroom and to correlate what she is discovering there with the experiences of those who teach the school's other writing courses. Of course, these discussions also give her a chance to acquaint the high school faculty with the principles underlying the university's freshman writing course. She supplements her in-class work and her informal discussions with an annual workshop in which she and the high school teachers compare essays written by students in the university's freshman writing course with essays written by students in the high school's upper-level writing courses. Then, the group develops strategies that will help the high school teachers better prepare their students for postsecondary work. The variety of ways in which the university teacher participates in the high school program—but especially her actually teaching a course there—contribute to the formation of a common frame of reference that interconnects the teaching of writing at the high school and at the university. And this common frame of reference is the key to meaningful articulation.

Paralleling the articulation efforts described above is a third program: a faculty member from ISU's English department has teamed up in the classroom with elementary school teachers to improve the reading and writing abilities of students in grades 2 through 6. The university teacher began this in-class work in a second-grade class during the fall of 1983, and she is continuing with the same group of students as third graders in 1984–85. She will follow this group of students through the sixth grade. Her participation in this project will not only help her see how students learn at particular levels but will also show her how they change and thus how they can best be taught over a series of five grades. One important difference between this project and the ones described above is that the visiting teacher and the host teacher are in the same class at the same time. This arrangement increases the opportunity for meaningful communication between them because their interaction always has a shared concrete context. Although teachers from different levels gain a common perspective on writing instruction when they teach one another's classes separately, they can learn more from each other when they work in the same classroom at the same time. As a team, they must solve specific and immediate teaching and learning problems, and as they work together to solve these problems, they necessarily teach each other something about how English can best be taught.

The NEH Collaborative Teaching Project

Various parts of all these programs have been combined to form the English department's most ambitious in-class school-college cooperative effort so far. With funding from the National Endowment for the Humanities, writing teachers at the university have completed a cooperative project with teachers from Illinois Central College and from three Normal-Bloomington high schools. The project again stresses the value of getting teachers from different grade levels into each other's writing classes at the same time so that they can develop a common frame of reference for discussing writing theory and pedagogy. This frame of reference then allows them to communicate more effectively about how writing instruction can best be approached in each class.

The NEH program began in the summer of 1983 and, though funding is scheduled to end in 1985, the project will continue in some form as long as it remains as successful as it has proved so far. It stresses the interaction among high school, community college, and university writing teachers because, although many programs emphasize the cooperative efforts of high school and community college teachers or of high school and university teachers, few recognize the value of bringing teachers from all three types of institutions together at the same time. In Illinois, many students go straight from high school to a four-year college or university while many others go to a community college, either to complete their education or to facilitate their later matriculation to a four-year college or university. Since writing teachers at all three types of institution deal with roughly the same group of students at different levels of development and in varied learning environments, the teachers at each level can add a unique and valuable perspective on the ways in which students' learning can be enhanced at any level.

The NEH program was divided into five parts, with each part designed to contribute in a special way to the formation of a common frame of reference capable of improving communication between secondary and postsecondary writing teachers. The first phase of the project stressed the importance of establishing a theoretical foundation for the teaching of writing. A myth informing some English articulation projects has it that high school teachers have a built-in antipathy toward anything too theoretical or too remote from the day-to-day concerns of teaching writing to adolescents. These projects then promote nuts-and-bolts activities that are not tied together by any conceptual framework. Most secondary teachers, however, are no more resistant to theory than are their post-secondary colleagues. They may ask harder questions of the theories they study, since they work in environments where research is less likely to be valued for its own sake; but as the high school teachers in this project demonstrated, they are clearly open to any theory that clearly improves their understanding of the process they teach and that enhances their ability to teach it.

Care was taken to ensure that the theories examined during this phase were broad enough and flexible enough to embrace and integrate the varied experiences and perspectives of the teachers from the different grade levels (high school sophomore through college freshman). Meeting throughout the summer of 1983, seven teachers from the four participating schools (Illinois State University, Illinois Central College, Bloomington High School, Normal Community High School, and University High School) met to read and discuss recent research in four areas: (1) writing as a process, (2) writing as a cognitive activity, (3) the correspondence between reading and writing, and (4) the relation between cognitive growth and the development of writing abilities. The first three focus on issues that should be addressed in any writing curriculum designed to have the greatest possible impact on students' writing abilities. The last area covers the principles involved in coordinating writing instruction across grade levels to help students "rework" their writing abilities as they learn to think more and more complexly in the course of their adolescence. From these workshops came both a new understanding of the curricular options open to teachers at all levels and—in some respects more important—a team approach to resolving curricular problems across grade levels.

The second phase of this project began in the fall of 1983 when the high school teachers and the community college teacher came to the Illinois State campus to coteach the university's required freshman writing course with the participating host teachers. In all, three sections of the course were used, so that no section would have more than three instructors. In addition to their in-class work, the teachers met weekly outside class to share perceptions about in-class activities and to develop as a group a curriculum suited to the specific needs of university freshmen. Thus, all discussions were carried on in the context of concrete learning problems that they had all experienced in their respective sections of the freshman writing course. This collaboration reinforced the integration of divergent perspectives that began the previous summer.

This phase placed a high priority on the development of a written curriculum, partly to give teachers a document that would help guide them in making curricular decisions during later phases of the project. More important, though, teachers were expected to write out the tentative curriculum they were developing because of the close correlation between writing and learning that has been stressed in recent composition research. To the degree that the teachers had to spell out the strategies they were formulating, they were forced to be more exact in their thinking than they would have been if they only had to verbalize these strategies in their group discussions.

During the third phase of the program, the participating university teachers went to the high schools and the community college to coteach selected writing courses at those schools. Because the project was designed to cover three high school grades, course assignments were distributed so that at one high school a host teacher and a university teacher taught the sophomore writing course, at a second the university teacher cotaught a junior writing and literature course with the host teacher, and at a third the cooperating teachers cotaught a writing course for college-bound seniors. In this way, all the project's high school grades were covered, but not at the same high school. This plan gave the teachers a more varied range of teaching and learning problems to draw on than they would have had if all the courses had been at a single high school. While this collaborative teaching was going on at the individual high schools, a university teacher also traveled to the community college to coteach the school's required freshman writing course with the teacher participating from that school.

Since the teachers had already worked together for a semester, they began the collaborative teaching in the high schools and the community college with a shared plan for teaching writing. Their task in this third phase was to accommodate the strategies they had already developed to the distinct needs of students in each of the high school and community college classes. This meant that each pair of teachers had to determine the level of thinking and writing development characteristic of their students and to find ways of cultivating students' writing abilities so that the students' thinking and writing would mutually enhance one another. Thus the succession of the project's courses would exhibit how writing instruction might gradually evolve from year to year to extend and refine students' thinking and writing abilities simultaneously.

Teachers also regularly met as a group outside class throughout the third phase, but instead of meeting every week they met about every three weeks, since they already had a model curriculum that could serve as a guide for the curricular decisions of each pair of teachers. The individual teams were encouraged, however, to challenge the model curriculum and to depart from it to the degree that their classroom experiences warranted. For example, all groups were to stress problem-solving assignments, starting students off with essays on subjective problems and gradually calling for papers on objective and academic questions. In practice, the students at the lower grade levels could not move from one kind of assignment to the other at the pace dictated by the curriculum. Each pair of teachers had to determine the pace appropriate to the students in the class. And, for reasons specified above, each team of teachers were again required to write out the curriculum they were developing. When they met in their group sessions, they discussed the changes they were making with everyone involved in the project. These group meetings, then, encouraged the teachers to continue to articulate the common set of curricular principles they had agreed on in earlier phases of the project and to develop an understanding of the different demands placed on these principles by students at different grade levels.

The fourth phase of the project took place during the summer of 1984 and required the participating teachers to meet and work as a group on a curriculum for each of the project's courses. Since they had developed a curriculum for each course through their collaborative teaching and through their meetings outside the classroom, they focused in this phase on refining and coordinating these existing curricula. In addition, they wrote teaching guides for their curricula so that teachers throughout Illinois who were not involved in the project could share in the common frame of reference developed through the collaborative teaching and reflected in the curricula the participating teachers wrote.

Each teacher was asked to work on the curriculum and teaching guide for the course that he or she hosted during the collaborative teaching. Because the participants had extensive experience teaching their respective courses, they could remain sensitive to the perspectives and experiences of those who taught similar courses at other schools, and at the same time they could approach those perspectives and experiences through the group's collective viewpoint. The teachers who received the project materials were therefore likely to find them familiar yet revolutionary. And the presence of the familiar would help make the revolutionary seem more accessible and reasonable. Writing up the final curricula and accompanying teaching guides also helped the teachers reconsider and clarify in their own minds the issues addressed throughout the earlier phases. Then, after the host teachers had completed this work, the whole group discussed the end products to see if they continued to reflect the curricular principles established in earlier phases of the project.

The curricula and teaching guides developed during this phase represent the major achievements of this project. Ultimately, getting teachers from different grade levels into each other's classes was a means toward an end, not an end in itself. The success of the project was measured by the degree to which this in-class cooperation led to positive changes in the teaching and learning that occur in the participants' individual courses and over the series of grade levels represented in the project. Starting with the research studied in the first phase of the project, the teachers began to think about new and more effective ways of teaching writing and thinking in their courses. By the time they wrote the final curricula and the teaching guides, they had learned to use problem-solving assignments that engaged their students more thoroughly and genuinely in the act of writing; they had learned how to help students identify appropriate roles, audiences, and purposes for the writing assigned; they had learned to help students develop practical invention and revision strategies for the writing process; they had learned how to teach students to make effective choices about everything from a text's structure to its grammar in the context of its purpose. Their curricula and teaching guides demonstrated that they had thoroughly assimilated this knowledge in their conceptions of what effective composition instruction entails. Moreover, because they worked as a team, they finished the project not with a series of discrete writing curricula but with an integrated sequence capable of effectively guiding the development of students' thinking and writing abilities over a series of secondary and postsecondary grades.

The project's fifth and final stage focused on evaluation. Evaluation strategies addressed two issues: (1) the degree to which the project's materials worked in the courses for which they were designed and (2) the degree to which teachers not involved in the project could readily use these materials. The methods of evaluation included administering before and after test essays to students enrolled in the project's courses during the first semester of the 1984–85 school year and distributing a series of questionnaires to teachers in high schools, community colleges, and universities throughout Illinois who were not involved in the project. At this writing, the results of the testing are not yet available; preliminary indications suggest, however, that the project has enjoyed substantial success in both respects.

Funding

Because cooperative teaching programs require the freedom of teachers to move from one school to another on a daily basis, funding can be a special problem. In the cooperative programs the department has sponsored so far, only the NEH project has required outside funding. The teacher exchange with Illinois Central College did not involve extra personnel costs, since both schools agreed to pay their representatives their regular salaries for the period. The only extra expenses incurred were travel costs, and the two departments covered these out of their regular budgets. When this teacher exchange is conducted again, however, the participating faculty members will probably be given more released time than they had earlier. Thus, the costs incurred are likely to include not only the extra travel expenses but the salaries needed to release each teacher from one course.

The programs at the local high school and at the elementary school require no extra expenditures. The high school and elementary school are too close to campus to require significant travel time and costs. There are no personnel expenses for these programs because the university does not have to replace the teachers involved in the two programs. Since the high school students must register at the university to be given credit for the course, the course is considered a part of the teacher's regular load. The teacher going to the elementary school teaches her normal load at the university and treats her time in the elementary school as research time.

The NEH project required outside funding primarily because many teachers were involved and because they had to work together outside as well as inside the classroom. Thus, the bulk of the project's budget went toward covering the costs needed to free the participating teachers from a portion of their regular duties. When teachers traveled to another school to coteach courses, the project paid to release them from forty percent of their obligations at their home schools. They were released from twenty percent of those duties during the semester in which they cotaught one of their regular courses with a visiting teacher. In addition to having time off for collaborative teaching, the directors of the project were released from twenty-five percent of their teaching load to administer the program. All teachers were also paid stipends for the work they completed during the summers in preparation for the following year's work. The other major expenses of the project were tied to its evaluation, and the principal items were copying costs and stipends for a team of independent evaluators.

Problems

The main difficulty with a collaborative teaching program is that it must be limited to a relatively small group of participants. Sharing the benefits with a larger group requires a special effort above and beyond the program itself. To involve more teachers in collaborative teaching, faculty members at Illinois State are considering ways to extend one or another kind of collaborative teaching arrangement to schools that have not directly participated in any of the programs so far. Moreover, those who have been involved in the programs so far are using workshops to disseminate the materials they developed and to discuss the effects of their participation on their teaching with others who teach writing courses at their grade levels.

A second problem: in any articulation program, teachers at different grade levels tend to regard one another with a degree of suspicion. Because collaborative teaching gets the teachers into the same classroom at the same time, this problem can be especially acute. There is always the danger that the host teacher will see the visiting teacher as an evaluator and will fear that he or she is being judged. If this suspicion is not diffused early in the program, it can make effective cooperation in the classroom virtually impossible by blocking the kind of open communication necessary to success. In the Illinois State program two methods of combating this danger have proved most effective: teachers have regularly met outside the classroom to discuss their experiences, and they have had frequent opportunities to get to know the collaborating teachers socially.

Finally, funding is always a problem. The collaborative teaching programs at Illinois State have been lucky enough to get initial support from the participating institutions and from the NEH. To sustain all aspects of the program, the English department has requested permanent financial support from the state for some of these activities. At this stage of the review process, the chances for success seem good. In fact, the university's board of regents and the Illinois Board of Higher Education have recommended the program for permanent funding, and the approval of the state legislature and the governor seems imminent. If the funding comes through, it will help to continue the programs we have developed so far and to move the concept of collaborative teaching in new directions.

Plans

We expect to develop the collaborative teaching program in three ways. First, with the funding that the English department hopes to receive from the state, faculty members will use the NEH model to work with additional secondary and postsecondary teachers in the state. Second, plans are now in the making for applying a modified version of this model to the College of Arts and Sciences' writing-across-the-curriculum program. Essentially, this modified program will bring together teachers of freshman-sophomore courses in the university's College of Arts and Sciences with those who teach the same subjects in high schools and community colleges around the state. Since teachers from sixteen schools and fifteen subject areas will participate, the main obstacles here are logistic. Finally, the success of the NEH collaborative teaching program in writing courses has encouraged the English department faculty to explore ways of adapting the model to the teaching of literature.

All of those who have participated in any aspect of the English department's collaborative teaching program have agreed that the experience was entirely different from anything they had experienced before. The major reasons for this feeling are the new approaches to writing instruction that they developed and the common frame of reference that has enabled them to understand the teaching and learning of writing more holistically than they did before becoming involved in the program. While the department fully intends to continue its out-of-class articulation efforts, its emphasis on communication through in-class cooperation has become a permanent feature of its work with high school and community college English teachers in Illinois.

Skidmore College: Cooperative Program in Cross-Curricular Writing

Philip P. Boshoff

In response to a request from Scarsdale schoolteachers who wanted to reinforce students' writing throughout the disciplines, the cooperative program between the Scarsdale Union Free School District and Skidmore College began in May 1983 as an extension of Skidmore's cross-curricular writing program.

In 1981–83 Mellon funds and a grant from the National Endowment for the Humanities (NEH) underwrote the costs for three 2½-week summer workshops on composition theory and teaching for Skidmore faculty members. The workshops enabled each participant to plan a new, discipline-specific writing course, to make an existing course more writing intensive, or to add writing components to an existing course. The workshop leaders, Phyllis Roth and Phil Boshoff of the Skidmore English department, designed and conducted the sessions to introduce their colleagues to differing theories of cognition (Benjamin Bloom, James Moffett, William Perry, Jean Piaget), composing (James Britton, Janet Emig, James Kinneavy, Lee Odell, Sondra Perl), language acquisition (A. R. Luria, L. S. Vygotsky), processes that writers use when composing (Donald Murray, Sondra Perl), and pedagogy (Lilian Brannon, Kenneth Bruffee, Toby Fulwiler, among others).

Workshop sessions emphasized daily interaction among participants, whom the leaders assisted in developing objectives for their courses and planning writing assignments and course syllabi. Other workshop activities provided opportunities for participants to simulate student roles as they shared their assignments and writing with colleagues, evaluated one another's assignments and writing, and responded to suggestions for revision. In short, throughout the workshop faculty members acquired practical experience with what they and their colleagues wrote, read, and planned to assign. The workshop leaders encouraged the participants to design assignments and courses that would make discipline-specific uses of writing and, if necessary, to adapt, change, or even discard the composition theory and pedagogy they discussed in the workshops. Participants were neither advised nor expected, therefore, to design clones of English composition courses.

As a result of these three workshops, a core of twenty-four faculty members at Skidmore currently use writing to help their students learn the content of courses that range from introductory surveys to senior seminars in seventeen disciplines: American studies, anthropology, art history, business, chemistry, dance, economics education, English, geology, history, mathematics, philosophy, psychology, sociology, sports studies, and theater. An important function of the NEH grant involved disseminating the assignments, curricula, and readings that participants designed in the workshops and tested in their courses to other colleges and to secondary schools. One such endeavor was a one-day workshop at the 1982 convention of the National Council of Teachers of English. Three Skidmore faculty members who had participated in the summer workshops (Penny Jolly, art history; Paul Corr, business; and Richard Lindemann, geology) and the two workshop leaders (Phyllis Roth and Phil Boshoff) conducted this workshop, which initiated the contact between faculty members at the college and teachers in the Scarsdale Union Free School District.

Structure

In May 1983, Phil Boshoff, director of expository writing; William Brynteson, chair of the history department; and Richard Lindemann, assistant professor of geology, were invited to conduct a day-long workshop at Scarsdale for junior and senior high school teachers and administrators. The workshop agenda included lectures about the uses of nongraded writing and heuristic devices in English, science, and social science; discussions about the cognitive and conceptual demands these fields made on students; and illustrations of the possible ways to sequence assignments and syllabi to reflect these demands. The workshop leaders and participants also discussed the problems that an instructor encounters when evaluating and responding to students' writing. The workshop concluded with an overview of the issues that Scarsdale teachers would like to consider in workshops during the school year.

Following this initial workshop, Adele Fiderer, a teacher and coordinator for curriculum development in the Scarsdale public schools; Judith Schwartz, an English teacher and coordinator of the Scarsdale Teachers Institute; and Phil Boshoff developed the syllabus and requirements for a writing-across-the-curriculum course that the Scarsdale Teachers Institute, an in-service program for faculty development, would fund. The course would meet between 4 October and 5 June for fifteen 2½-hour sessions. Twelve junior and senior high school teachers enrolled, representing English, mathematics, science, and social studies. Two learning-skills specialists at the junior high took the course.

Fiderer, Schwartz, and Boshoff planned the course to be more than simply a learn-from-a-lecture-by-an-expert model; therefore, they incorporated many strategies from the Skidmore faculty workshops into the Scarsdale course, such as having teacher participants exchange reading material and assignments, evaluate them in peer conferences, and simulate student-teacher roles with one another's assignments. Because they assumed that the participants, experts in the demands of their own disciplines, would learn more by taking active roles in the course meetings than by just listening to lectures, they asked participants to lead discussions on topics of their choice. The course would also serve as a support group in which instructors could develop assignments and discuss such practical concerns as grading problem papers, establishing grading criteria for writing assignments, and finding effective ways to incorporate writing into their courses. The participants would conduct, or coconduct, ten sessions, and in addition to leading five discussions, Boshoff would meet one day every other month with teacher participants and other faculty members and administrators at the junior and senior high schools.

Fiderer and Schwartz decided that teachers participating in the course would receive two or three salary credits from the Teachers Institute. To receive two credits, each instructor would attend ten sessions and complete three of the following projects; to receive three credits, each instructor would attend fifteen sessions and complete any five of the following projects:

1. Write a course or unit outline integrating writing assignments into the syllabus. (Two teachers can work together on this project.)
2. Design six writing assignments, three of which include prewriting strategies and develop their demands sequentially in order of increasing complexity, making all hidden agendas explicit.
3. Develop a file of good student writings with instructor's comments.
4. Write a two-page critique of any two books in the bibliography, paying special attention to the sections that are most helpful for writing instruction.
5. Lead, or colead, one of the sessions. Provide handouts and pertinent readings for participants. [All participants led at least one session.]
6. Keep a course journal for the year noting experiences, responses, and observations as you and your students adopt writing strategies.
7. Design and implement an independent study project of your choice. (Discuss plans in advance with Fiderer and Boshoff.)
8. Write a proposal for a project that will further a cross-curricular writing program. Some possibilities include the following:
   • Work with students to prepare a handbook on writing strategies for your discipline.
   • Devise a plan for using peer tutors in one of your classes.
   • Work with colleagues in your department to intensify the writing expectations in another course.
   • Establish a writing support file for teachers in your department, including examples of writing assignments, course objectives, evaluation techniques, and models of effective and ineffective student writing.
   • Prepare an annotated bibliography of at least ten books or articles about teaching writing that would be helpful for your department.
   • Write a brief document for teachers in your discipline entitled "How to Design Effective Writing Assignments in ———," "Hints for Grading Writing in ———," "Problems Students Have When They Write in ———," etc.
   • Write a proposal for a workshop, panel, or paper for the National Council of Teachers of English (NCTE) conference, the Conference on College Composition and Communication (CCCC), the New York State College English Association conference, or the Modern Language Association (MLA) convention.

Course requirements would have to be completed and certified by the institute and forwarded to the personnel office within ninety days after the course was completed. Fiderer and Boshoff would review all assignments.

After surveying the teacher participants' interests, Fiderer, Schwartz, and Boshoff planned the following topics for discussion during the course:

Oct. 4   Journal Writing for Discovery
Nov. 8   Improving and Expanding Techniques for Responding to Student Writing
Dec. 13   Strategies for Designing Clear Writing Assignments

Jan. 10   Using a Newspaper Format to Promote Writing in Civic Education
Feb. 14   Notebook Writing in Mathematics and Science
Mar. 13   The Uses of Holistic Evaluation in Checking Assignments and Establishing a Grading Range
Apr. 10   Adding Writing Components to Social Studies Courses

In September, at the first meeting with Boshoff, the participants compiled a list of six other topics for meetings, based on their discussion of the common problems teaching writing in their courses would pose:

1. Sequencing Writing Assignments Developmentally
2. Devising Heuristic Techniques for Problem Solving
3. Making Effective Use of Student Models
4. Teaching Editing Skills Effectively
5. Helping Students with Reading and Note-Taking
6. Reporting on Research on Writing across Disciplines and Planning Future Projects

As the participants discovered after a couple of meetings, their working together on these projects also raised other issues. Chief among these was the recognition of the need for junior and high school teachers to discuss problems common to their teaching and curricula. Many instructors at Scarsdale felt that too little substantive communication occurred among the junior and senior high staffs. They discovered that many high school administrators and instructors based their course expectations and curricula on what material they assumed junior high school teachers had assigned. Thus the course encouraged teachers at both schools to develop assignments and curricula that built on material from previous courses. When discussing theories of cognition, for example, participants worked on applying Bloom's taxonomy to sequencing assignments at several grade levels. And thinking about their course expectations in terms of the cognitive skills they wanted their students to attain gave them new perspectives on the clarity and sophistication of their assignments. Many seventh- and eighth-grade students, for example, were unlikely to attain Perry's stage of commitment on any but the most basic, dichotomous issues. In another instance, a junior high school English teacher and a social studies teacher reshaped their assignments to move students away from confronting only simple dualities. The English teacher introduced her students to contradictory editorial opinions about candidates in a primary election. She then asked them to summarize their opinions about the candidate, which they followed with a rebuttal based both on their own observations and on the readings.

By the end of the course, all twelve teacher participants had completed projects that they will discuss with their colleagues, share with administrators, present at conferences and workshops, and continue to research and test. Their projects cover a range of curricular, pedagogical, and rhetorical issues. One participant will develop a student advisory group on writing. Several participants established files of students' essays, which they would use four ways: to show other students possible ways of approaching a topic, to give students "stuck" on an assignment a boost, to provide teachers with examples of discipline-specific writing assignments, and to give teachers and students examples of essays they can evaluate. Another instructor wrote a proposal for including more writing in the ninth-grade civic education course. An English teacher developed a scheme for linking the visual arts to a ninth-grade poetry unit. A mathematics teacher reported on using a notebook in her geometry class. Next year she plans to focus students' notebook writing on the problem-solving strategies they use to prove theorems. She will also assign process essays in which students explain to someone not in the course how to construct geometric figures with specific angles and dimensions that fit into areas with spatial constraints. Before taking the course, she had relied on objective tests and a few short-answer questions. Her students remarked in evaluations that they had enjoyed applying the geometric facts to real-world problems.

In another discipline-specific assignment, a junior high school social studies teacher asks students to imagine themselves involved in the westward expansion and to keep a journal of their experiences. He also gives students audience-specific writing tasks: a letter to a member of the clergy describing the religious practices of Native Americans and other settlers, a letter explaining methods of barter and exchange to a banker, or agricultural practices to a farmer, or military practices to someone at West Point. By specifying audiences, he helped his students avoid the "random dump" of providing undifferentiated factual information; they had to sort through what they had read and select the information most pertinent to their audience.

A junior high school science teacher had students submit drafts of a grant proposal requesting funds to develop energy sources other than electricity and fossil fuels. Students worked on the essay throughout the first four months of classes. They generated topics, prepared drafts, checked a peer's draft and then their own with self- and peer-assessment sheets, revised their drafts in the light of their peers' suggestions and new information, and repeated self- and peer-evaluation before submitting a final draft. The instructor was amazed at how readily students were willing to make large revisions on their drafts, and he felt the finished essays were his best set since he had been teaching the course. This instructor, a department chair, intends to collaborate with colleagues on ways to integrate writing and revising into the junior high school science curriculum.

Three participants from English made effective use of journals and reading guides to increase their students' comprehension of literature. One of these instructors attended an NEH 1984 summer seminar on the teaching of writing to develop further uses for student journals in literature courses. Three participants and Boshoff discussed the projects developed in the teacher's institute at the spring 1985 CCCC meeting. Two participants talked to a Scarsdale parents group about effective methods for home tutoring. And in September 1985, Amy Levin began a writing center at the high school, which is staffed by high school students who are trained to tutor their peers.

To further the collaboration between the Scarsdale Union Free School District and Skidmore College, course participants visited the Skidmore campus in April 1985 to sit in on cross-curricular writing classes, confer with Skidmore faculty members, observe tutoring in the college writing center, and talk with Skidmore administrators about future collaborative programs. Another endeavor being discussed is a student-teaching project between Skidmore and Scarsdale in English and cross-curricular writing at the elementary and junior high schools. The plans are for a student teacher to teach in the classroom and to work jointly with Fiderer and Boshoff in developing curricula and designing writing components for courses. Other plans under discussion include a possible summer workshop for elementary, junior high, and high school teachers that Skidmore faculty members and Scarsdale teachers will offer jointly. And a longitudinal study is being set up at Scarsdale to track elementary students who were enrolled in writing-intensive classes against elementary students who had traditional, non-writing-intensive courses, to measure the effect of early writing instruction as both groups move through the grades.

Although collaborative activities in 1984–85 did not include another Scarsdale Teachers Institute class, teachers from the 1983–84 course have formed a writing committee to plan and coordinate future activities, primarily those that require working with other teachers on developing writing assignments for integration into courses. Boshoff made bimonthly trips to the school district to continue working with members of the core group and to conduct in-service workshops with faculty members in the history and English departments. The 1984–85 Scarsdale School District budget funded this endeavor. The central goal of the 1983–84 course was to establish a nucleus of teachers and administrators as in-house consultants for Scarsdale teachers. Our experience suggests that the more a school district relies on its own staff to administer and conduct a program, the greater the acceptance. Collaborative activities during the 1985–86 year will center on individual departments. Boshoff and other Skidmore faculty members will discuss the ways in which faculty members in specific disciplines grade papers; specifically, they will discuss their criteria for A, B, and C papers.

Problems

Although the response from Scarsdale administrators, course participants, and students to the cooperative program was overwhelmingly favorable, several problems came to our attention. Chief among them were the reluctance of some high school faculty members to commit time to the course and their unwillingness to add writing to their existing courses. They believed that teaching writing detracts from the substance of a course that demands numerous classes before students master difficult concepts. This reluctance was especially apparent among teachers of junior and senior chemistry, history, and mathematics courses. While high school faculty members encouraged junior high school teachers to integrate writing instruction into their courses, they also argued that their more demanding courses were too overburdened with content to include writing.

Another problem was not unique with Scarsdale's program. As most coordinators of cross-curricular writing programs discover, some instructors balk at modifying their time-honored and often successful teaching methods. In a highly competitive, affluent school district, one in which nearly one hundred percent of the seniors attend college, administrators and teachers are often reluctant to change curricula and pedagogy. Moreover, because students and parents prize grades, many instructors object to assigning ungraded writing. By repeatedly stressing the benefits of writing as a process to help students learn course material, we overcame some, but not all, of this resistance. We specifically encouraged the participants who assigned course notebooks and who worked with students through several drafts of essays to discuss the ways in which having to recall, analyze, synthesize, and evaluate course readings and problems helped students clarify ideas, rethink assignments in the light of the new material, and master course content. Our most persuasive arguments for administrators and department chairs were based on the increased emphasis on cross-curricular writing in both scholarship and practice. The numerous accomplishments in cross-curricular writing at a variety of small and large private and public secondary schools and colleges demonstrated that writing across disciplines is not merely a limited educational fad.

Recommendations

Our experience suggests that teachers from disciplines other than English must be involved in conducting workshops to show how rhetorical theory and pedagogy can be adapted for the aims of their curricula. Any successful collaborative program must make use of, or at least include, key personnel at the college and secondary schools: department chairs, administrators, influential faculty members, and especially successful, inspired teachers. When planning a collaborative program, we have found it helpful to consider the benefits that the endeavor will have both for the college and university and for the secondary school or schools. Many colleges and universities draw their students primarily from neighboring cities or geographic regions; but institutions like Skidmore, which has few students from its immediate vicinity, logically establish collaborative programs with their feeder schools, not with the local schools.

In designing the collaborative sessions, we found that assigning participants ongoing projects is worthwhile. Such tasks might begin by establishing immediate goals and move to setting less readily attainable, perhaps ideal, goals. Once instructors feel relatively comfortable including some writing instruction in their courses, they have established classroom-tested methods on which to build. For example, two instructors from the Scarsdale course have centered their ninth-grade social studies course sequence on aspects of Perry's developmental schemata. In another instance an English teacher has team-taught a course with an art instructor. Both devised ways to tap students' affective responses in prewriting strategies designed to connect their visual sensitivities to their verbal expression. The hope is that the students' aesthetic perceptions will develop along with their writing skills.

Our experience has also revealed that encouraging participants to be active professionally sparks their enthusiasm for the program. Thus we encouraged teachers to submit paper proposals, to plan meetings with other colleagues, and to interact with other school systems. We have also learned not to dismiss instructors who initially seem threatened by, or hostile to, some aspects of the "new" rhetoric. Often their arguments can open productive opportunities for discussion and debate. Finally, we offer two suggestions: first, program leaders—to be most productive and least threatening—should act as consultants, as collaborators, and not as authoritarians; second, college and university faculty members should be responsive to the problems that secondary teachers face, recognizing that what they offer these teachers are suggestions, not panaceas. In short, we must be willing to give up riding a cherished hobbyhorse when others refuse to ride along.

Works Cited

"An Articulated English Program: A Hypothesis to Test." *PMLA* 74 (1959): 13–19.

Berthoff, Ann E. *The Making of Meaning: Metaphors, Models, and Maxims for Writing Teachers.* Montclair: Boynton, 1981.

Boyer, Ernest. Foreword. Maeroff. vii–x.

——. *High School: A Report on Secondary Education in America.* New York: Harper, 1983.

Commission on English. *College Preparation in English: A Working Paper (1960).* New York: MLA, 1964.

——. *Preparation in English for College-Bound Students (1960).* New York: MLA, 1964.

Cooper, Charles. Foreword. *Writing in the Secondary Schools: English and the Content Areas.* By Arthur Applebee. Urbana: NCTE, 1981. xi–xiii.

Dixon, John. *Growth through English: A Report Based on the Dartmouth Seminar.* Reading, Eng.: National Assoc. for the Teaching of English, 1967.

"EQuality Project Links Collaboratives." *Academic Connections* Winter 1984; 1–3.

Hairston, Maxine. "The Winds of Change: Thomas Kuhn and the Revolution in the Teaching of Writing." *College Composition and Communication* 33 (1982): 76–88.

Heller, Erich. *The Artist's Journey into the Interior.* New York: Vintage, 1965.

Krashen, Stephen. "Second Language Acquisition." *Personal Viewpoints on Aspects of ESL.* Ed. M. Burt et al. New York: Regents, 1976.

Maeroff, Gene. "Ties That Do Not Bind." *Change* Jan.-Feb. 1982: 12–17.

——. *School and College: Partnerships in Education.* Princeton: Carnegie Foundation for the Advancement of Teaching, 1983.

Modern Language Association of America. Commission on the Future of the Profession. "Working Paper of the Commission on the Future of the Profession, May 1981." *PMLA* 96 (1981): 525–40.

National Council of Teachers of English. Committee on High School–College Articulation. "High School–College Liaison Programs: Sponsors, Patterns, and Problems." *English Journal* 51 (1962): 85–93.

National Science Foundation and United States Department of Education. *Science and Engineering Education for the 1980's and Beyond.* 1980.

O'Keefe, Michael. "High School/College Cooperative Programs." *Current Issues in Higher Education* ns 1 (1981): 5–10.

Papert, Seymour. *Mindstorms: Children, Computers, and Powerful Ideas.* New York: Basic, 1980.

Rockefeller Commission on the Humanities. *The Humanities in American Life.* Berkeley: U of California P, 1980.

Rogers, Robert. "Articulating High School and College Teaching of English." *English Journal* 54 (1965): 370–74.

Sachs, Murray. "Collaboration's End: 'Live in Fragments No Longer.'" *Profession 84* (1984): 41–43.

"Six University Presidents Call for Closer Ties with Public Schools." *Chronicle of Higher Education* 31 Aug. 1983: 5.

United States. Dept. of Education. Commission on Excellence in Education. *The Nation at Risk: The Imperative for Educational Reform*. Washington: GPO, 1983.

Watkins, Beverley. "Colleges Urged to Help Schools Improve Students' Preparation." *Chronicle of Higher Education* 27 May 1980: 1, 14.